Between two Unions

Europeanisation
and Scottish devolution

Manchester University Press

DEVOLUTION series

series editor Charlie Jeffrey

Devolution has established new political institutions in Scotland, Wales, Northern Ireland, London and the other English regions since 1997. These devolution reforms have far-reaching implications for the politics, policy and society of the UK. Radical institutional change, combined with a fuller capacity to express the UK's distinctive territorial identities, is reshaping the way the UK is governed and opening up new directions of public policy. These are the biggest changes to UK politics for at least 150 years.

The *Devolution* series brings together the best research in the UK on devolution and its implications. It draws together the best analysis from the Economic and Social Research Council's research programme on Devolution and Constitutional Change. The series will have three central themes, each a vital component in understanding the changes devolution has set in train.

1 **Delivering public policy after devolution, diverging from Westminster**. Does devolution result in the provision of different standards of public service in health or education, or in widening economic disparities from one part of the UK to another? If so, does it matter?

2 **The political institutions of devolution**. How well do the new devolved institutions work? How effectively are devolved and UK-level matters coordinated? How have political organisations which have traditionally operated UK-wide – political parties, interest groups – responded to multi-level politics?

3 **Public attitudes, devolution and national identity**. How do people in different parts of the UK assess the performance of the new devolved institutions? Do people identify themselves differently as a result of devolution? Does a common sense of Britishness still unite people from different parts of the UK?

already published

Territorial politics and health policy
UK health policy in comparative perspective
Scott L. Greer

Between two Unions

Europeanisation and Scottish devolution

Paolo Dardanelli

Manchester University Press

Manchester and New York

distributed exclusively in the USA by Palgrave

Copyright © Paolo Dardanelli 2005

The right of Paolo Dardanelli to be identified as the author of this work has been asserted by him in accordance with the Copyright, Designs and Patents Act 1988.

Published by Manchester University Press
Oxford Road, Manchester M13 9NR, UK
and Room 400, 175 Fifth Avenue, New York, NY 10010, USA
www.manchesteruniversitypress.co.uk

Distributed exclusively in the USA by
Palgrave, 175 Fifth Avenue, New York,
NY 10010, USA

Distributed exclusively in Canada by
UBC Press, University of British Columbia, 2029 West Mall,
Vancouver, BC, Canada V6T 1Z2

British Library Cataloguing-in-Publication Data
A catalogue record for this book is available from the British Library

Library of Congress Cataloging-in-Publication Data applied for

ISBN 0 7190 7080 5 *hardback*
EAN 978 0 7190 7080 8

First published 2005

14 13 12 11 10 09 08 07 06 05   10 9 8 7 6 5 4 3 2 1

Typeset by Servis Filmsetting Ltd, Manchester
Printed in Great Britain
by CPI, Bath

7 Day

Contents

Figures and tables

Figures

Tables

Acknowledgements

This book started life as a doctoral thesis for the London School of Economics and I owe a very great deal to the encouragement, support and assistance I received from many people and institutions for a number of years. The Economic and Social Research Council and the Department of Government of the London School of Economics awarded me Research Studentships (ESRC No. R00429824368), without which the research on which this book is based would have never been completed. I am grateful to the policy-makers who agreed to be interviewed and to the librarians and archivists who endured my requests, in particular Sean Townsend of the LSE Data Library, Elizabeth Canning of the STUC archive in Glasgow and Sarah Charlton of the House of Commons. For valuable comments and suggestions, I am indebted to the organisers and participants of the UACES Annual Conference in Glasgow in January 1999, the UACES workshop in Belfast in June 2000 and the ECPR Joint Sessions in Grenoble in April 2001 as well as to the convenors and participants in the doctoral workshops at the LSE, in particular Antonia Dodds, Claire Sutherland, Lee McGowan, Eiko Thielemann, Howard Elcock, Michael Keating, Pieter van Houten, Rodney Barker, 5ebastian Balfour, Abby Innes and Chris van Stolk. Simon Hix, George Jones, James Mitchell, Joanne Wright, Charlie Jeffery, Thomas Saalfeld and Clive Church, as well as the staff and referees at Manchester University Press, have read parts of the book or the whole of it and have given me scholarly advice and personal encouragement for which I am most grateful to them. I would also like to thank my fellow PhD students at the LSE with whom I shared the PS2/3 research room and all the difficult and joyous moments of doing doctoral research, in particular: Thibaut Kleiner, Leonidas Makris, Susana Berruecos, Francisco 'Chico' Gaetani, Geeta Kulshrestha, Razmik Panossian, Zhand Shakibi, Adam Tebble and Nebojsa Vladisavljevic. My thanks also go to Marco and Kaori Costantino, Stefano and Manuela Saldini, Edoardo and Silvia Faganello and Daniela Orsetti who offered friendship and understanding throughout these, sometimes difficult, years. Wendy Jenkins was by my side for most of the time offering support and much more which was of great help in completing this work. Finally, my deepest thanks are to my parents, Matteo Dardanelli and Giovanna Altana, who first taught me to love the pursuit of knowledge and have offered unwavering support ever since.

Some of the material in chapters 4, 8 and 10 appeared previously in Democratic Deficit or the Europeanisation of Secession? Explaining the Devaluation Referendums in Scotland. Political Studies 53/2: 320–42 (2005).

Canterbury
January 2005

1
Introduction

European integration and devolution of power to the regional level are two of the most important phenomena which have affected the European states over the last thirty years. Their taking place more or less simultaneously has naturally raised the question of whether there is a causal connection between them, i.e. whether the process of supra-state integration generates or increases demands for regional self-government which lead to processes of regionalisation.

The question has been present in the literature for a long time, with the first works addressing it published in the mid-1970s[1] but no rigorous theoretical and empirical analysis of the impact of the European dimension on a case of demand for regional self-government has, to my knowledge, so far been conducted. There are numerous suggestions that there is indeed a positive causal relationship between European integration and demands for regional self-government but these suggestions are not substantiated by robust empirical evidence against alternative hypotheses. It could thus be said that the existing literature keeps raising the question without providing a satisfactory answer.

The present work intends to provide such an answer by analysing the case of Scottish devolution. Scotland provides an ideal test case for the general hypothesis that European integration raises demand for self-government at sub-state level for three main reasons. First, the establishment of a Scottish Parliament is the most recent and arguably the highest-profile case of demand for self-government at regional level in Europe. Second, there is a long history of demand for self-government in Scotland, which thus allows for testing the impact of European integration as an additional variable or, as the title of this book suggests, how membership of the European Union affected membership of the British Union. Third, the existence of two very distinctive periods – culminating in the referendums of 1979, which failed to show sufficient support for devolution, and in 1997, when the result was decisively in favour – allows for a comparison across time in presence of change in both the independent and the dependent variable. The objective of the book is thus to investigate to what extent the development of the European Union[2] affected the demand for self-government in Scotland and, more particularly, whether the deepening of European integration between 1979 and 1997 had a causal effect on the different results of the two devolution referendums. The book does this through a cross-time comparison between the periods 1974–79 and 1988–97, each culminating in a referendum.

The book shows that Europeanisation of Scottish self-government failed in the 1970s but succeeded in the 1990s and that this variation was a key causal factor in the different outcomes of the two devolution referendums. It argues, however, that the indirect impact of Europeanisation, via support for independence, was stronger than the direct impact on support for devolution. Moreover, variation over time was more a result of elite actor agency than of the deepening of European integration. These results offer an alternative explanation for the failure and success of devolution in the 1970s and 1990s and shed new light on the key theoretical question of the connection between European integration and demands for regional self-government.

The remainder of the book is organised into ten chapters grouped in three parts. Chapters 2 to 5 in Part I analyse the degree to which the demand for self-government in Scotland at the elite and mass level was Europeanised in the 1970s, focusing in particular on political parties, interest groups and public opinion. Chapters 6 to 9 in Part II perform a similar analysis with regard to the 1988–97 period. Chapter 10 in Part III explains the different degree of Europeanisation of the two periods and summarises the theoretical conclusions of the present work. The last chapter looks to the future and tries to predict how the European dimension will affect the future of self-government in Scotland.

Theories of the demand for regional self-government

As mentioned above, the demand for regional self-government in advanced democratic states has attracted substantial scholarly interest since the 1960s. As a result, there is now a vast body of literature on this topic. In this section, I intend to give the reader a brief overview of the main contributions to this literature and of its theoretical 'state-of-the-art'. For the sake of analytical clarity, I divide the discussion into two sub-sections – regionalism and regional nationalism on the one hand and secession on the other – though this distinction is not always clear-cut in the literature. Before turning to the literature, however, it is necessary to define the terms 'region' and 'self-government' that are central to this book. By region, I refer to the largest territorial units within a state possessing some characteristics of distinctiveness, beyond a purely geographical nature. If it possesses some political or administrative features, it is the political unit immediately below the central level. In this usage region is not opposed to nation but to state. I conceptualise Scotland as both a region and a nation, the former in legal-political terms, the latter in historical and iden-tificational terms. As regards the demand for self-government, I define it as a demand for part or for all of the powers hitherto exercised at the central level to be transferred to the regional level. This demand usually takes two main forms: 'autonomous' or 'devolved' self-government and independent self-government. Following the British usage, the terms 'devolution' and 'devolved self-government' are used throughout to refer to self-government within the existing state structure.[3]

Regionalism and regional nationalism

Three broad causal determinants of regional demands for self-government have been identified in the literature: sociological factors, economic factors and political factors. Depending on where the emphasis is placed, one obtains three approaches: cultural-sociological, economic-instrumentalist and a political one. The first two are structure-centred approaches in which empha-sis is placed on cultural and economic structural factors whereas the latter emphasises actors' agency and treats cultural and economic elements as largely exogenous. The three approaches also differ from one another in the degree to which they include the extra-state dimension in their analysis.

The cultural-sociological approach sees the demand for regional self-government – often termed 'ethno-nationalism' – as primarily determined by cultural distinctiveness of a given region relative to the rest of the state, usually in terms of ethnicity, language, religion or some combination of them. It sees the phenomenon as the continuation of the rise of nationalism over the last two centuries and downplays the role of both economic factors and elite agency. The extra-state dimension is only relevant as far as a 'demon-stration effect' between different countries is concerned. The most elaborate version of this model has been put forward by Walker Connor, the very initiator of the term 'ethno-nationalism'.[4] Birch advanced an 'internal critique' of this thesis, based on a rationalist framework. He argues that the demand for self-government is triggered by a reassessment of the perceived costs/benefits of the status quo and that this changes over time, notably because of changes in the international environment. Other authors falling in this category acknowledge the importance of the external dimension but disagree as to its effect on regional demands.[5]

Economic models contrast cultural explanations with the primacy of economic factors. They conceptualise the demand for self-government as a reaction to economic imbalances between different areas of a state. If these areas coincide with regional units with a distinctive character, then economic factors are expected to compound cultural ones and to produce demand for regional self-government. Hechter's 'internal colonialism' thesis was among the first to employ this approach.[6] Also in this category, falls what I would call the 'new growth' model, which sees demands for regional self-government fuelled by the role accorded to the latter in the new theories of economic development, based on endogenous factors and regional micro-intervention. The external environment, in the shape of globalisation, plays an important role in this model while it does not feature prominently in Hechter's.[7]

To a large extent, most empirical approaches to cases of demand for self-government give a crucial role to political agency such as party strategies and focus on how and when these actors mobilise the underlying structural elements of a cultural or economic nature.[8] Leifer first pointed out the inadequacies of explanations based only on cultural or economic structural factors and pointed to the crucial role of political leadership. In a similar vein, is the work by Smith, Thompson and Rudolph and, more recently, Lecours on the conditions under which the politicisation of regionally based cultural and economic cleavages occur.[9] Newman and Van Houten take this approach further by focusing on the role of political parties in particular.[10] Although these models are agency-centred, they do not neglect structural factors such as the extra-state dimension. Van Houten has moved in this direction with an attempt to analyse the connection between globalisation and demands for regional self-government though he has not clearly identified a causal connection between the two.[11]

Secession

The study of secession has traditionally been conducted within normative political theory – generally focused on the moral justifications for it. Only relatively recently has secession been approached from a positive perspective with the aim of arriving at a positive theory of secession. The first attempt to devise an explanatory model of secession was Wood's comparative exploration which identified a series of preconditions to a demand for secession and emphasised the catalytic role of a coherent movement with a defined ideology, a solid organisation and effective leadership.[12] Hechter and Dion take this approach further in a rationalist direction and attempt to explain why secessions are rare events and, indeed, have never taken place in established democracies. They stress the 'interface' between structural factors, elite agency, state response and the international environment in the dynamics of secession.[13]

Meadwell also adopts a rationalist approach but places greater emphasis on institutionalist variables such as decentralisation and power-sharing and he applies them to the Quebec case in particular. He takes the external dimension into account and argues that it has, in different ways, strengthened support for secession in Quebec.[14]

Studies of the propensity to secession in the former Soviet Union by Emizet and Hesli and Hale, on the other hand, find that economic factors were the strongest determinants.[15] More broadly, Polèse and Bookman also focus on the economic dimension to secession. Their models share a view of secession as dependent on a calculation of the economic costs and benefits of independence compared with those of devolution or the status quo.[16] While these models focus primarily on the internal dimension, the 'free trade' model of secession is explicitly centred on the external dimension. With contributions from both economists and political scientists, its central claim is that economic integration based on free trade is a facilitator of demands for independence because it lowers the economic costs of secession. On the assumption that support for independence is influenced by rational calculations of costs and benefits, it predicts that economic integration generates pressures for political disintegration.[17]

In the most comprehensive analysis of secession currently available, Bartkus proposes a rationalist model accounting for the decision to secede based on four variables: benefits and costs of membership in the state, on the one hand, and benefits and costs of secession on the other hand. Benefits and costs are understood as being both material and ideational, in the economic, political and cultural spheres Secession is explained on the basis of a perceived shift in the relative balance of the four variables. The extra-state dimension plays a central role in this model, as the shift can be determined by changes at both 'the level of the state and of the international system'.[18]

Two main points emerge from this briefest of reviews of the literature on the demand for regional self-government. First, that over time a consensus has been reached on the underlying factors and the emphasis has shifted onto political variables such as elite agency. Second, that the external dimension is an important aspect and that, in particular, the nature of the international economic environment can have a crucial effect. The following section reviews the literature dealing with the process of Europeanisation.

Theories of Europeanisation

This section reviews the literature on Europeanisation and, in particular, that on the Europeanisation of the demands for regional self-government. It shows that attention to the connection between the two phenomena has long been present in the literature, that a number of hypotheses have been advanced but that no detailed theoretical and empirical study has yet been conducted. Although the subject-matter of Europeanisation is as old as the process of European integration, the term 'Europeanisation' itself has only recently gained wide acceptance to refer to the 'domestic impact' of integration.[19] The most elaborate general conceptualisation of Europeanisation put forward sees it as a phenomenon generated by a 'misfit' between the properties of the EU system – be they in the field of policy, politics or polity – and the properties of the domestic system. This misfit produces pressures for change at the domestic level which represent opportunities and constraints for domestic actors as they affect both the distribution of resources among them as well as their norms and identities. Depending on the institutional properties of the domestic system and the strategies of domestic actors, the impact of Europeanisation can vary widely.[20]

Europeanisation and state structures

Although the literature on Europeanisation has so far concentrated mainly on the impact on public policy, a few studies have addressed the question of the extent to which Europeanisation has affected the relationship between the state and the regions in the member states. Most of these studies found that Europeanisation has a discernible impact on the vertical distribution of power within the state, although there is no agreement on whether this impact is positive – i.e. strengthening the regional level – or negative, while some authors argue that there is no significant impact.

Among the latter, Dehousse does not mention the state–regions dimension in his study of the impact of European integration on the states, while Kohler-Koch argues that Europeanisation does not change the constitutional situation in the member states though it does influence the way the government process is carried out.[21] Among the former, Ladrech made the centre–periphery relationship one of the two case studies of his work on the Europeanisation of the French political system and found that the single market contributed to demands for economic planning at the regional level and that the EU regional policy provided additional legitimacy to such demands.[22] Goetz addressed the same questions in the German context and found that Europeanisation did not alter the overall structure of German federalism but that it did have a significant impact on the balance of power between the state and the regions.[23] In the most recent and most comprehensive of these studies, Börzel reaches broadly similar conclusions. She argues that Europeanisation tends to weaken the regions but that they may have the resources to successfully fight back. Among the latter, an additional factor is the normative values of the 'Europe of the Regions' idea which regions can use to legitimise their demands vis-à-vis the state.[24]

If the impact of European integration on the internal structures of the member states is largely absent from the classical theories of integration, neo-functionalism and (liberal) intergovernmentalism, it is central to the 'multi-level governance' (MLG) conceptualisation of the EU system. While the idea that the European Union is a multi-level political system in which a central 'state' level co-exists with increasingly powerful 'supra-state' and 'sub-state' levels is not new, the MLG concept has attracted considerable interest over the last ten years.[25] The MLG model, advanced by Marks and his collaborators, describes an EU system in which increasing transfers of power upwards to the Union take place side by side with transfers of power downwards to the regional level and, crucially, in which the upper and lower level increasingly deal directly with each other by-passing the middle – i.e. state – level. This process is not a neat, zero-sum redistribution and thus produces a fluid, MLG system in which power is increasingly dispersed and negotiated vertically between the three levels and horizontally between each of three levels and non-governmental actors, leaving no clear central locus of power.[26] Direct contacts between the sub- and supra-state levels are most likely to take place in the area of the structural funds and through regional 'mobilisation' to gain a presence in Brussels and to build trans-state networks.[27]

Europeanisation and demands for regional self-government

Like the concern for the impact of European integration on state structures, the question of the Europeanisation of demands for regional self-government has been present in the literature since the mid-1970s, when Feld, for example, asked 'will politics for regional autonomy be linked to European politics?'[28] Since then, this question has been addressed by a large number of authors, from different perspectives and with different conclusions, though this review shows that it has never been subjected to a rigorous theoretical and empirical analysis. The contributions to this strand of the literature can be divided into three broad categories, depending on how they interpret the connection between the two phenomena and the predictions they derive from them.

In the first group are those who see Europeanisation as weakening demands for self-government, as exemplified by Scheinman. He perceived a clear connection between the two phenomena but saw them as potentially contradictory, primarily because integration was controlled by state governments and because the capitalist character of the EU was inimical to regionalist demands for cultural and economic protection.[29] The middle group is made up of those who see the two phenomena as being largely independent of one another, because regionalist demands are generated by cultural conflicts with deep historical roots which usually pre-date the process of integration and are largely unaffected by it. Moreover, the most powerful actors at the Union level are state governments, which leaves purely supra-state institutions such as the Commission and the Parliament with not enough power and decisional autonomy to strategically use the process of integration to encourage demands for self-government at the regional level.[30] Most of the authors who have written on Europeanisation of regionalist demands fall in the third category of those who perceive a positive connection. At the most general level, they argue that integration has reduced the role of the state in the policy process and undermined the principle of absolute state sovereignty thus opening the way to demands for self-government from the regions. Integration is likely to proceed hand in hand with pressures for state fragmentation.[31] More specifically, they identify a number of causal mechanisms through which the European dimension can lead to Europeanisation of demands for regional self-government.

Among those focusing on institutional factors, Birch points out that the EU offers the guarantee of a large market and, especially, a favourable institutional structure for regions contemplating secession.[32] Others argue that the principle of subsidiarity provides a powerful 'European' legitimation to regionalist demands and that the establishment of the Committee of the Regions creates an incentive for acquiring a governmental capacity at the regional level.[33] In the late 1970s, Rudolph saw the first direct election to the European Parliament as offering the regions an incentive to acquire self-government so as to exploit the Parliament as an arena in which to pursue their strategies by-passing the states.[34]

A great deal of attention has been paid to the Europeanising effect of the structural funds, especially after their reform in 1988. By involving regional administrations in the management of the funds, the reform is seen as having offered the regions a strong incentive to acquire governmental capacities in order to maximise their chances of securing and efficiently managing the funds. Some authors have gone as far as suggesting that fuelling demands for self-government at the regional level was an explicit objective of the Commission's strategy to strengthen its position vis-à-vis the state governments.[35] More generally, this vision is central to the literature on multi-level governance discussed above though empirical studies have found remarkably little evidence supporting this hypothesis.[36]

As regards the economic factors, two connections have been identified. The first is that the increased constraints placed on the ability of central governments to intervene in the economy has generated a powerful incentives for regional action.[37] The second focuses on the single market and sees it as a structure that, by guaranteeing free trade and regulatory continuity, reduces the economic costs of secession – along the lines of the literature discussed in the previous section.[38]

Finally, several authors have argued that European integration also affects the symbolic sphere of the demand for self-government in two main ways. First, the emergence of the European Union generates a shift in identification away from the states and towards both Europe and the regions. In that scenario, regions would attract stronger identification and thus offer an opportunity to self-government 'entrepreneurs' to politicise and mobilise that identity for their ends.[39] Second, the idea of a 'Europe of the Regions' provided a powerful legitimation of the demands for self-government at regional level by making them appear a natural counterpart to the process of European integration.[40]

Three main conclusions emerge from the review conducted in this section. First, there is an increasing interest in the domestic impact of European integration, under the broad heading of Europeanisation. Second, most of the theoretical contributions to this literature see a potential positive effect of Europeanisation on regionalist demands and focus on the structural funds as the key causal mechanism. However, third, the studies that have set out to test the impact of the structural funds have found limited effects while the European dimension of other demands for regional self-government has not been thoroughly investigated. The following section reviews the literature dealing with the Scottish case.

Demand for self-government in Scotland

In this section, I first give a brief historical overview of Scotland's constitutional position within the United Kingdom and of its demand for self-government, including both devolution and independence. Subsequently, I review the literature dealing with the two periods which are the object of this study and with the results of the two referendums in 1979 and 1997 in particular. The last section reviews the role assigned to the European dimension in such a literature.

Brief historical background

Scotland became united with England in 1707 when the Scottish and English kingdoms, and their respective parliaments, merged to establish a United Kingdom of Great Britain.[41] Despite the creation of a single Parliament Scotland secured the right to maintain its own institutions of the Presbyterian Church of Scotland, the legal and educational systems and local government under the terms of the Treaty/Act of Union.[42] After having experienced some troubles in the first half of the eighteenth century, the union became fully accepted in Scotland and self-government was not an issue until the 1880s. At that time it emerged for the first time as a political issue as a result of the debate on the Irish question and Gladstone's proposal for Irish home rule.[43] The central government response was to go some way towards accommodating Scotland's demands without compromising parliamentary sovereignty and political control over public policy. The way chosen to do so was to establish in 1885 a territorial department to deal with Scottish affairs – the Scottish Office – headed by a Scottish Secretary of ministerial rank. The Scottish Office was to run the administration for Scotland and its secretary to be the 'voice of Scotland in government' and the 'voice of government in Scotland'. Notwithstanding the establishment of the Office, the demands for self-government did not go away and a number of bills to establish home rule were introduced to Parliament in the 1910s and 1920s. These came to nothing, though they may have contributed to the decision to move the Scottish Office administration from London to Edinburgh in 1939.

In 1945, the Scottish National party (SNP) – which had been created in the 1930s – won its first ever seat in a by-election for the Motherwell constituency. A few years later, in 1949, a Scottish Covenant demanding a devolved Parliament attracted around two million signatures – out of a total Scottish population of five million. The first ever opinion poll on the issue, conducted in 1947, found a three-quarters majority in favour of self-government. However, in 1958 the Labour party in Scotland reversed a long-held support in principle and adopted a policy of opposition to devolution. Over the post-war years, the broad lines of the territorial arrangement remained essentially the same, though with the significant change that over time, as a result of relative demographic and economic decline, Scotland became over-represented in the House of Commons and the beneficiary of disproportionate public spending. Meanwhile, the SNP vote rose steadily throughout the 1960s and early 1970s, from 0.5 per cent in 1959 to close to 21.9 per cent and 30.4 per cent in the two 1974 elections, respectively, with high-profile victories in former Labour strongholds such as Hamilton in 1967 and Glasgow Govan in 1973.

A commission of inquiry into the phenomenon of regional demands for self-government – the Royal Commission on the Constitution or Kilbrandon Commission after the name of its last chairman – reported in 1973 with a majority recommendation for a directly elected Scottish Assembly. For the October 1974 general elections the three main UK-wide political parties published for the first time a separate Scottish manifesto and committed themselves to some form of Scottish Assembly. With the SNP vote at

30 per cent and eleven MPs, the Labour government elected in October 1974 made devolution to Scotland – and Wales – a central plank of its programme. It published two white papers in 1975–76 and introduced a bill to Parliament in 1976 to establish devolved assemblies in Scotland and Wales which, however, fell victim to a defeated guillotine motion in February 1977. After a tactical agreement with the Liberal party, later that year the government introduced a second bill – this time specific to Scotland – which became the Scotland Act 1978. Due to pressure from anti-devolutionists from its own ranks as well as from those of the opposition, a clause was incorporated into the Act making the latter's implementation subject to endorsement by at least 40 per cent of the Scottish electorate in a referendum. The referendum was held on 1 March 1979 and resulted in 51.6 per cent Yes and 48.5 per cent No on a 62.9 per cent turnout, which translated into 33 per cent of the electorate endorsing the Act against 31 per cent rejecting it. These figures falling far short of the required threshold, the implementation of devolution was effectively blocked and the Act was later repealed by the incoming Conservative government.

The referendum defeat and the concomitant decline of the SNP vote removed the issue of Scottish self-government from political centre-stage until the late 1980s though the issue remained alive in Scotland. In 1988–89 a Claim of Right for Scotland asserting the sovereignty of the Scottish people to decide Scotland's government was signed and a year later a broadly based Constitutional Convention was launched. Over the same period, the SNP adopted a policy of secession from the UK but with membership of the European Union under the slogan 'Independence in Europe'. The Convention's first report, presented in 1990 and calling for a Scottish Parliament, became official policy of the Labour party, which promised to implement it after gaining office. The Convention's final report in 1995 was again adopted as official policy by Labour which also decided to put the issue to a referendum after the next general election but before legislation was produced, thus on the basis of a white paper. After the 1997 Labour victory, a white paper was promptly published and a two-question referendum held on 11 September 1997. The first question asked whether voters agreed that there should be a Scottish Parliament, while the second question asked whether the Parliament should have tax-varying powers. The result was 74.3 per cent to 25.7 per cent in favour of a Parliament and 63.5 per cent to 36 per cent in favour of tax-varying powers on a 60.2 per cent turnout. In 1999 the first election for the Scottish Parliament was held and the Parliament convened for the first time.

Existing explanations

This section reviews the existing explanations for the results of the two referendums in 1979 and 1997. As no explicitly comparative work exists, I review the literature dealing with each of them in turn.

There is broad consensus that the result of the 1979 referendum was the product of a rapid shift in public opinion, although different authors attribute it to different causes. Balsom and McAllister identify the decline in support among Conservatives as the key cause and they relate it to the partisan nature of the Act and the decline of the SNP.[44] Butler and McLean and Watt hypothesise that dissatisfaction with the Labour government after the 'winter of discontent' must have played a role.[45] Perman focused on the campaign itself and argued that the Yes camp lost the referendum because it was divided and contradictory in its arguments.[46] Brand fully accepts the thesis of polarisation but he reckons that the result was the product of a rejection of devolution in general not just of the Scotland Act 1978.[47] Bochel and Denver argue that support for devolution was 'soft' and was thus easily undermined by the more effective No campaign and the declining popularity of Labour and the SNP.[48]

Two main studies of the 1997 referendum have so far been published. Though neither of them explicitly intends to compare the 1997 referendum with the 1979 one, the second study in particular contains many comparisons between the two.

The first study, by McCrone and his collaborators, emphasises two main points: the shift in the social pattern of support for self-government and the expectations about public policy and democracy at the time of the second referendum. They first point out that the middle classes had mainly voted No in 1979 while the only social group opposed to devolution in 1979 was constituted by those identifying with the Conservative party.[49] Secondly, they stress that the 1997 referendum result can be understood as a product of rational voting on the part of voters seeking improved public services and greater democracy.[50] Another perspective, put forward by Paterson, explains the higher demand for self-government in 1997 as a result of the mobilisation of the Scottish middle class as a reaction to the threat to Scottish civil society represented by Conservative policies over the period 1979–97.[51]

Denver and his collaborators focus on three main 'contingent' differences related to the specific devolution proposals and the circumstances of the vote and on two broader 'background' factors.[52] They first point out that the white paper of 1997 was an improved document compared to the Scotland Act 1978 because it was offering a wider degree of self-government – including taxation powers – and a fairer electoral system, thus making devolution much more appealing to a broad range of voters.[53] Secondly, Labour and the broader Yes side was much more united than in 1979 – hence the success of the Constitutional Convention – while the business community's decision not to actively take part in the campaign, left the No side dependent only on the resources of a weakened Conservative party.[54] Thirdly, but in their eyes most importantly, in 1997 devolution was associated with a popular government and a popular prime minister – the reverse of the 1979 situation. This gave a positive image of the devolution proposals and added credibility to the Yes campaign.[55] Beyond these circumstantial differences, however, Denver et al. see the crucial difference arising from deeper and longer-term trends, including a growing primary identification with Scotland and the effect of the 1979–97 'democratic deficit'.

Concentrating on broad trends, Brown et al. see three factors producing changes in the politics of self-government between 1979 and 1997. First, a growing concern with the quality of democracy and its relation with government effectiveness.[56] Secondly, the 'democratic deficit' created by successive British governments with only very limited support in Scotland[57] and, lastly, 'the slow reorientation of Scotland towards the EU and away from Britain'.[58] I discuss this last point in the sub-section below.

The European dimension

Of the three main studies reviewed above, only the one by Brown et al., sees a significant influence of the European dimension. The other two focus exclusively on domestic factors.

Brown, McCrone and Paterson argue that the 'growing importance of the EU' was an important factor in the evolution of the politics of self-government between 1979 and 1997.[59] They point to four main aspects. First, the EU was attractive for the SNP because it 'provides a new framework of external security and trading opportunities to replace the UK'.[60] Second, it was also attractive for the parties supporting devolution because 'the EU favours subsidiarity' and subsidiarity was used by pro-devolution actors to support their argument for devolution of power within the UK.[61] Third, they claim that 'Europe' has assumed the role of a source of modernising and progressive ideas that was once England's. Lastly, they also point out that the EU appeared 'close to the welfare-state consensus that Scotland seems to favour' when this was under attack from the Conservative government in the UK.[62] In a sociological study, Hearn also argues that Scottish nationalism has been influenced by the European dimension because 'the steady growth of the European Union has both eaten into the sovereignty of the British state, and made the viability of small nations within the EU seem more plausible, and Scottish independence less isolationist'.[63]

Conceptualising Europeanisation of the Scottish demand for self-government

In this section I present and explain a model of the connection between the two phenomena with two cases and three levels of analysis. The comparison is conducted over time between Scotland in the period 1974–79, with focus on the 1979 referendum, and Scotland in the period 1988–97, with focus on the 1997 referendum. These are the 'static' periods in which the positions of the actors and their strategies were largely fixed. The period in between – 1979–88 – is a 'dynamic' one, for a number of changes in the EU and UK structures as well as among Scottish actors took place. Figure 1.1 offers a

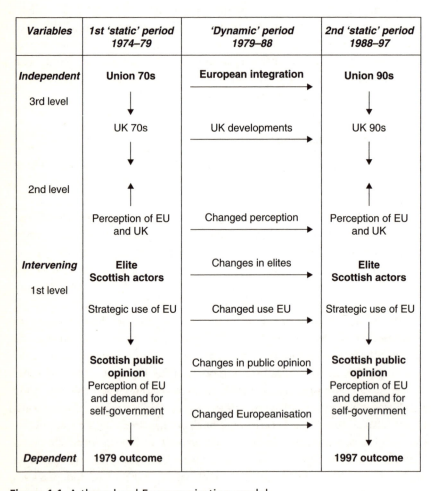

Variables	1st 'static' period 1974–79	'Dynamic' period 1979–88	2nd 'static' period 1988–97
Independent 3rd level	Union 70s ↓ UK 70s ↓	European integration → UK developments →	Union 90s ↓ UK 90s ↓
2nd level	↑ Perception of EU and UK	Changed perception →	↑ Perception of EU and UK
Intervening 1st level	**Elite Scottish actors** Strategic use of EU ↓	Changes in elites → Changed use EU →	**Elite Scottish actors** Strategic use of EU ↓
	Scottish public opinion Perception of EU and demand for self-government ↓	Changes in public opinion → Changed Europeanisation →	**Scottish public opinion** Perception of EU and demand for self-government ↓
Dependent	1979 outcome		1997 outcome

Figure 1.1 A three-level Europeanisation model

graphic representation of the model with its *levels*, *dimensions*, *variables* and *mechanisms*. I discuss each of these aspects below.

Levels

In each of the three periods, the model captures Europeanisation as a process operating across three levels – Union, UK, Scotland – of the multi-level EU system, with each level conceptualised as a political structure. The upper layers of the graph represent the two wider levels while the bottom layer represents the regional level nested within the state and the Union. At the bottom layer, one finds both elite actors and the mass public.

Dimensions

The model has two basic dimensions: a vertical and a horizontal one. The vertical one – the 'columns' of the graph – represent the impact of the European Union on the demand for self-government at mass public level – via elites' perceptions and strategies – in each of the static periods and, in particular, at the time of the two referendums in 1979 and 1997. At those points in time the properties of the variables, both the structural levels and the actors, were fixed. As the model is concerned with testing hypotheses, its main dimension is the 'comparative statics' of the two cases: 1979 and 1997. The horizontal one – the 'rows' of the graph – represent the dynamic dimension of the changes in the independent and intervening variables over time that influence the variation in the dependent variable. I use this dimension to explain the changes in the variables between the two points in time.

Variables

The model has three sets of variables: independent, intervening and dependent. There are two independent variables: the United Kingdom and the European Union. Variations in the properties of either or both of these variables are assumed to have been necessary in producing – via the intervening variable – variation in the dependent variable. The UK variable is linked to the 'null hypothesis' while the EU is linked to the 'operative' hypotheses discussed below. By this I mean that the model assumes that variation in the dependent variable was entirely caused by variation in the UK variable, unless the analysis indicates that EU variables had a significant causal effect. As the burden of proof is on the role of the EU, the latter is the key 'operative' variable and the analysis is focused on its static and dynamic properties. The model is not concerned with explaining the origins and the determinants of the Scottish demand for self-government prior to the 1970s. It treats them as exogenously given and focuses on the relative influence of the UK and EU factors as they were in the 1970s and the 1990s.

The intervening variable is the agency of the elite Scottish actors in Scotland, with focus on parties and interest groups, who acted as a crucial 'hinge' between the UK and the EU structures and public opinion. Both of these elite actors had motives to support or to oppose self-government, were able to influence each other and public opinion and were in a position to utilise the European dimension to increase support or opposition to self-government at mass public level. Lastly, the model treats the demand for self-government at mass public level as the dependent variable, the one that – as expressed in the two referendums – ultimately decided the outcome of the politics of self-government at the end of the two periods under examination.

Mechanisms

Europeanisation can be said to have had a significant impact on the demand for self-government in Scotland if factors related to the EU had a significant influence in the outcomes of the two referendums. With the aim of ascertaining whether this was the case, I conceptualise the EU as having properties which provided incentives and opportunities or placed constraints on regional self-government. Hence, Europeanisation occurred if the properties of the EU system were perceived by elite actors as raising the benefits and reducing the costs of self-government and if this effect was used by them to re-shape the distribution of preferences at mass public level. In order for this to happen, the model assumes that public opinion is significantly shaped around core preferences by elite actors with a central role played by parties. This means that the ideal points of voters' preferences are likely to be determined exogenously but that elite agency – notably in referendum campaigns – can significantly shift such preferences around core ideal points. These shifts can be enough to determine the difference between success and failure in referendum votes. This follows established models of elite shaping of preference formation at public opinion level put forward, among others, by Ward and Zaller.[64]

I conceptualise the dependent variable as being public demand for self-government because it ultimately decided the fate of devolution. To be successful, elite positions had to be translated into mass public demands. By demand for self-government I mean support for constitutional options involving varying degree of self-government, i.e. devolution and independence, as expressed by answers to opinion poll surveys and votes in the referendums. The relevant options were essentially two: devolution or home rule and independence. The two options could be kept distinct as far as opinion polls were concerned but not when it came to the referendum vote as independence was not on offer. The referendum vote was thus determined by a complex combination of attitudes to devolution and attitudes to independence, with two features: the shape of the preference order between status quo, devolution and independence and the existence of an interaction effect between the latter two, as discussed in greater depth in chapter 4.

Hypotheses

On the basis of the above model, it is possible to generate a number of hypotheses on the Europeanisation of the demand for self-government in Scotland. I divide these into three categories: one null hypothesis, four macro-hypotheses and seven micro-hypotheses. The macro-hypotheses relate to the broad general connection between the EU and the demand for self-government. The micro-hypotheses relate to a number of mechanisms through which I hypothesise such connection actually took place. To capture the static and dynamic properties of the EU, each of the micro-hypotheses includes a description of both dimensions. In the case of the macro-hypotheses, the first three – coded A–C – conceptualise static mechanisms and the last one – coded D – conceptualises the broad dynamic one. The null hypothesis is as follows:

N   The demand for self-government at both elite and mass public levels, as expressed in the referendum results in 1979 and 1997, was not significantly affected by the European dimension.

Against this null hypothesis, the study tests the following macro-hypotheses:

A   Elite political actors demanding self-government for Scotland perceived the European Union as providing opportunities and incentives that improved the costs/benefits balance of self-government vis-à-vis the status quo
B   They strategically used such opportunities and incentives to raise the demand for self-government at mass public level:
C   Public opinion's demand for self-government was increased as a direct result of the utilisation of European elements in the strategy of elite political actors.
D   The deeper integration of the European Union in 1997 relative to 1979 had a significant influence on the endorsement of devolution in 1997 as opposed to its rejection in 1979.

To operationalise these macro-hypotheses it is necessary to identify which elements of the EU were perceived as improving the costs/benefits balance of self-government relative to the status quo and through which mechanisms they operated. In order to do so I dis-aggregate the macro-hypotheses into a set of micro-hypotheses. For the sake of clarity, I have divided them in two groups according to a primary impact on devolution or on independence, respectively. To each of these hypotheses can be opposed a null hypothesis that the connection hypothesised did not take place or worked in the opposite direction, i.e. reducing benefits or raising costs.

BENEFITS AND COSTS OF DEVOLUTION

1   EU policy-making created the need for Scottish representation at that level. It offered an incentive to acquire self-government, on the assumption that the latter was necessary for effective representation. Dynamically, the widening of policy-making responsibilities at the Union level increased the saliency of representation and thus sharpened the incentive to acquire regional government.

2   The constraints placed by membership of the European Union on the UK government's intervention in the economy created the need for policies at the Scottish level. The EU thus offered an incentive to acquire self-government on the assumption that the latter was necessary if those policies were to be both effective and accountable. Dynamically, the tightening of such constraints increased the urgency of action at the Scottish level.

3   The structural funds created the need for autonomous and accountable actors at the Scottish level to manage them. They thus provided an EU-derived incentive to acquire self-government on the assumption that the latter was necessary to manage the funds both effectively and democratically. Dynamically, the growth of the funds and their reforms raised the profile of the issue.

4   Membership of the supra-national EU undermined the monolithic conception of state sovereignty and legitimated the devolution of power to the regional level. It thus offered the opportunity to argue that devolution was the logical counterpart to the shift of power to the European level. Three dynamics are relevant here. First, the EU's elements of supra-nationality deepened with the increased use of majority voting and the granting of a legislative role to the European Parliament. Second, the idea of a Europe of the Regions gained mainstream acceptance and led to institutional innovations – the Committee of the Regions and the principle of subsidiarity – reinforcing the legitimation of regional self-government. Third, closer contacts with other states possessing a regional level of government created a 'demonstration effect' towards 'institutional isomorphism'.

BENEFITS AND COSTS OF INDEPENDENCE

5   The existence of free trade and of a customs union across the EU reduced
     the economic costs to Scotland of seceding from the UK but remain-
     ing within the EU. Membership of the EU thus provided a powerful
     opportunity to improve the costs/benefits balance of independence
     vis-à-vis devolution and the status quo. Dynamically, the completion of
     the single-market programme increased the degree of integration of the
     EU's internal market hence further reducing the economic costs of
     secession.

6   The bias in favour of small states in the EU institutional structure and the
     pre-eminence of the Council of Ministers and of the European Council
     gave a structural advantage to a 'state' status vis-à-vis a 'region' status.
     They thus offered Scotland a powerful incentive to acquire statehood.
     Dynamically, the expansion of the EU policy-making remit increased the
     attractiveness of such benefits.

7   Membership of the EU generated a shift in popular identification away
     from the UK and towards both Europe and Scotland. This provided an
     opportunity to reduce the affective costs involved in seceding from the UK
     and the increase in identification with Scotland bolstered the legitimacy of
     the independence claim. Dynamically, the deepening of integration
     further increased identification with Europe and reduced identification
     with the UK.

Conclusions

Supra-state integration and sub-state regionalisation are prominent phenomena affecting contemporary European states. Both have attracted keen scholarly interest and generated vast bodies of literature. One key theoretical
question found in this literature is whether there is a causal connection
between the two phenomena, notably in the direction of integration fuelling
demands for regional self-government. Despite the fact that this question has
often been raised, it has not yet been properly answered as no systematic
analysis of the impact of the European dimension on a prominent case of
regionalisation has so far been conducted. More generally, the impact of the
extra-state dimension is under-explored in the literature on regionalisation,
not least because there has been little cross-fertilisation between the different
strands of the literature that touch upon this question while a robust analysis
of the impact of European integration on the demands for regional self-
government needs to draw from all these contributions.

The purpose of the present work is to address these issues and questions with the two-fold objective of shedding light on a prominent case of regionalisation – Scotland – and on the general theoretical question. Scotland is an ideal test case for several reasons, notably because the demand for self-government pre-dates the UK's entry into the EU and because of the presence of two distinct phases, each culminating in a referendum, which allows for a cross-time comparative analysis. Despite this, the literature on the demand for self-government in Scotland lacks an explicitly comparative study of the two referendums in 1979 and 1997 while existing works largely neglect the influence of the European dimension.

The book is based on a theoretical model that conceptualises Europeanisation as a three-level process. Properties of the EU political system – the independent variable – present opportunities, incentives and constraints for elite actors at the state and the regional level – the intervening variable – who in turn utilise them to influence public opinion, in particular in relation to the referendum votes – the dependent variable. A cross-time comparative analysis allows for identifying which features of the EU system had a potential impact on the demand for regional self-government, whether and to what extent elite actors utilised them and to what extent their actions had an impact on public demand for devolution.

The central findings are that the politics of Scottish self-government was not significantly Europeanised in the 1970s, primarily because elite actors demanding self-government had a negative perception of the EU system, on ideological grounds essentially. Failure to exploit the European dimension and the fact that devolution was linked to the prospect of independence meant that in the eyes of public opinion, devolution was linked to the prospect of secession and the latter was deeply feared. As a result of an interaction effect between attitudes to devolution and attitudes to independence, voters rejected devolution in the 1979 referendum even though more than 60 per cent of them supported self-government in principle. In contrast, the SNP, Labour and the other pro-self-government elite actors had a positive attitude towards the EU in the 1990s and extensively exploited the European dimension in their strategies. Their campaigning strategies profoundly reshaped public opinion, notably in dramatically raising support for independence within the European Union. The fact that independence overtook the status quo as 'second best' among constitutional options neutralised the interaction effect and led to a strong endorsement of devolution in the 1997 referendum. Hence, the degree of Europeanisation was a crucial determinant of the different outcomes of the two referendums. Within it, ideological and strategic change among elite actors, more than the evolution of the EU system, account for most of the variation.

Notes

1 See Rhodes (1973–74), Feld (1975), Rudolph (1977).
2 For the sake of clarity and consistency, I use the terms 'European Union' and 'EU' to refer to both the present EU and to what in the 1970s was variously called the EEC, the European Communities and the Common Market.
3 See Dardanelli (2002: 9–11) for a wider discussion of the concepts of region and self-government.
4 See Connor (1977, 1984 and, more generally, 1994); see also Petersen (1975) and Horowitz (1981).
5 Nagel and Olzack (1982) and Parks and Elcock (2000) identify a positive effect whereas Hannan (1979) sees it as reinforcing regions' loyalty to the state.
6 Hechter (1975).
7 See Mény (1986: especially 3–6), Rhodes (1995: 6–7), Keating (1988: 147–66), Armstrong (1997).
8 See Gourevitch (1979: 303–7), Smith (1979), Kolinsky (1981: especially 86), Rothschild (1981: especially 248–58), Rokkan and Urwin (1982), Kellas (1991: 228) and Sharpe (1993: 7).
9 See Smith (1982), Thompson and Rudolph (1989) and Lecours (2000).
10 Newman (1996) and Van Houten (2001).
11 Van Houten (2003); on the influence of the external environment see also Orridge (1982) and Orridge and Williams (1982).
12 Wood (1981).
13 See Hechter (1992) and Dion (1996).
14 Meadwell (1999, 2001).
15 See Emizet and Hesli (1995) and Hale (2000).
16 See Polèse (1985) and Bookman (1993).
17 See, in particular, Meadwell (1989, 1993), Martin (1995), Meadwell and Martin (1996). Among the economists, see Wittman (1991), Alesina and Spolaore (1996; 1997), Alesina and Wacziarg (1997), Bolton and Roland (1997).
18 Bartkus (1999).
19 Early examples of *ante litteram* Europeanisation studies are Wallace and Wallace (1973) and Rhodes (1973–74).
20 See Börzel and Risse (2003).
21 See Dehousse (1996) and Kohler-Koch (1998: especially 19).
22 Ladrech (1994: 80–5).
23 Goetz (1995: especially 105); see also Jeffery (1994).
24 Börzel (1999: 575).
25 For early conceptualisations of the EU as a three-level political system, see Rhodes (1973–74), Feld (1975) and, especially, Rudolph (1977).
26 See, among others, Marks (1992; 1996), Marks, Hooghe and Blank (1996), Hooghe and Marks (2001).
27 For a concise exposition, see Hooghe and Marks (1996) and a similar analysis in Borras-Alomar et al. (1994). On the regional offices in Brussels, see Feld (1975), Hooghe (1995), Jeffery (1996) and Marks, Salk, Ray and Nielsen (1996).
28 Feld (1975: 1192).
29 Scheinman (1977).

30 See, among others, Kolinsky (1981: 86–94), Urwin (1982), Sharpe (1993: 2), De Bandt (1992).

31 Rudolph (1977: esp. 544) was a pioneer of this interpretation; for more recent discussions, see Kellas (1991: 226–31) and Keating (1992).

32 Birch (1978: 336).

33 See Ladrech (1994: 82) and Jones (1995: 294–5) and Anderson and Goodman (1995: 617), respectively.

34 Rudolph (1977: 555).

35 See Hooghe (1996); Tömmel (1998).

36 For the theoretical formulation, see, among others, Marks (1992), Nanetti (1996) and Hix and Goetz (2000: 11) though the hypothesis was first formulated by Rhodes (1973–74: 68), Feld (1975) and Rudolph (1977: 554) in the 1970s. For empirical testing, see Anderson (1991), Martin and Pearce (1993), Garmise (1997), Smyrl (1997), Bache and Jones (2000).

37 See Keating (1993: 308), Cheshire (1995: 27), Rhodes (1995: 8), Anderson and Goodman (1995: 614–20).

38 See Keating (1995: 7–8), Bolton and Roland (1997: 1066).

39 See Rudolph (1977: 554), Kolinsky (1981: 96), Maxwell (1991: 151), Keating (1992: 48), Sharpe (1993: 35), Anderson (1994: esp. 12–13).

40 See Anderson (1991: 420), Borras-Alomar et al. (1994: 1).

41 The two countries already had the same sovereign since 1603; for a concise overview of the circumstances of the union, see Davies (1999: 533–657).

42 The document is usually referred to as the Act of Union in England and as the Treaty of Union in Scotland. Its text is reproduced in Davies (1999: 1139–40).

43 From this point onwards, the section draws on Bogdanor (1999: 110–43 and 166–200).

44 Balsom and McAllister (1979); see also Miller (1980: 112–18), Brown et al. (1998: 21) and Denver et al. (2000: 22).

45 Butler and McLean (1999: 7) and Watt (1979: 146); see also Mitchell (1996: 163) and Kellas (1999: 225).

46 Perman (1979: 54); see also Mitchell (1996: 163–4), Mitchell et al. (1998: 167), Denver et al. (2000: 19).

47 Brand (1986: 38).

48 Bochel and Denver (1981: esp. 144–6).

49 Surridge and McCrone (1999: 44).

50 Ibidem: 47.

51 See Paterson et al. (1992: especially 634) and Paterson and Wyn Jones (1999).

52 See Denver et al. (2000: 15; 75).

53 See Mitchell et al. (1998: 168) and Pattie et al. (1998: 8).

54 See Mitchell et al. (1998: 175–7), Pattie et al. (1999: 141–2), Denver et al. (2000: 75–6).

55 See Pattie et al. (1998: 14–15) and Denver et al. (2000: 49).

56 Brown et al. (1998: 62).

57 Ibidem: 64.

58 Ibidem: 64.

59 Ibidem: 22, 64–5.

60 Ibidem: 22, 64–5.

61 Ibidem: 22–3.
62 Ibidem: 23.
63 Hearn (2000: 5).
64 See the 'preference-shaping' model of party competition in Ward (2000) and Ward and Dunleavy (1981, 1991) and Zaller (1992: esp. 40–52 and 310–32).

Part I
THE 1970s

2
Political parties

Political parties were the most important elite actors in the politics of Scottish self-government. Where parties stood on the spectrum of constitutional options, what perceptions they had of the European dimension and how they played their strategies are crucial factors in assessing their impact on the distribution of preferences at public opinion level. In this chapter I analyse such factors in relation to the Scottish National party (SNP), the Labour party and the Conservative party, the three main actors of the Scottish party system and the protagonists in the politics of self-government.[1] What is now the Liberal Democratic party has been excluded from the analysis for three main reasons. Firstly, the other main parties represented the three distinctive policies on self-government that were the object of electoral competition in Scotland while the Liberals'/Liberal Democrats' preferred option of a federalised UK was never seriously debated. Secondly, electoral studies have shown that Liberal Democrats attract in Scotland a disproportionate number of 'protest' votes thus making support for the party rather disconnected from support for its policies, notably on self-government. Thirdly, the party's policy on self-government enjoyed a low level of visibility among the electorate, so the party is unlikely to have been effective in influencing public opinion.[2]

The chapter shows that the pro-self-government parties had a hostile attitude towards the European Union, did not perceive the European dimension as significantly affecting their positions and largely failed to exploit it in their strategies. Their Conservative opponents adopted a policy of supporting devolution in principle but opposing the Scotland Act 1978 in practice and centred their strategy on the risk that devolution would lead to secession and the contradictions within the Yes camp between Labour and the SNP.

The Scottish National party

The Scottish National party grew rapidly from the late 1960s to become the third party in Scotland in October 1974 when the party polled

30.4 per cent – its best result ever – and secured eleven seats. The SNP vote then declined sharply in 1979, when the party lost all but two of its MPs and attracted 17.3 per cent of the popular vote.

Self-government policy

The SNP was the single most important actor in the politics of self-government for it had been the party's rise which turned Scotland's constitutional status into a mainstream political issue. The issue has, of course, always lain at the core of the SNP's policies, as the party's raison d'être is to acquire sovereign statehood for Scotland.[3] In the 1970s, this goal was defined as independence under the British Crown and within the Commonwealth but, as discussed below, outside the European Union. Traditionally, the party intended to pursue this goal by gaining the majority of the Scottish seats in the House of Commons and, on that basis, claim a popular mandate to negotiate Scotland's secession from the UK. This policy rested on three conceptual points. First, the assertion of Scotland's status as a nation and its consequent inalienable right to self-determination. This assertion implied a conceptualisation of the UK as a partnership between the Scottish and the other three nations rather than a fusion of them to create a British nation. Second, a negative perception of the historical experience of union with England, primarily because of the threat to Scotland's survival as a distinctive nation. Third, the conviction that with the end of the British Empire and the discovery of oil in the Scottish section of the North Sea, it was no longer in the economic interest of the Scottish nation to belong to the United Kingdom.

If the party had a clear objective and solid (at least in its own eyes) reasons to pursue it, the central problem was to go through the steps described above and, in particular, gain a majority of Scottish seats. This appeared indeed very difficult for the party to achieve. Even after the electoral triumph in the October 1974 general election, the party still controlled only eleven out of seventy-two seats. In this context, the emergence of the Labour party's policy to establish a Scottish Assembly created an acute strategic dilemma.[4] On the one hand, an assembly could be seen as providing an excellent opportunity for the SNP. In a purely Scottish electoral competition the likelihood of the party gaining a majority of seats was arguably higher than in a UK-wide competition such as for a general election. Moreover, once having obtained control of a Scottish Assembly, the party would have been in a position to claim an even stronger popular mandate for seeking secession from the UK. On the other hand, with popular support for independence still very low, there was a high risk that a devolved assembly would satisfy Scots' demand for self-government thus depriving the SNP of its key competitive argument and making the prospect of independence an even more distant one. In other words, 'that the establishment of a Scottish Assembly might satisfy the electorate sufficiently to postpone the achievement of independence indefinitely'.[5] In this logic, a preference for the status quo over devolution would have made sense for the party on the ground that the maintenance of the former would have been the best way of fuelling support for independence. The party was split along these two interpretations of the connection between devolution and independence into 'gradualist' and 'fundamentalist' wings. The latter shared the second view of devolution and believed that the party should stick to the traditional policy of gaining a majority of Scottish MPs, while the former had a positive view of devolution and wanted to use an assembly as a stepping-stone to secession. They thought that the prospect of the SNP gaining a majority of Scottish seats was, at best, a distant one and anything that could have made Scots more accustomed to the idea of self-government had to be welcomed.[6]

Though the conflict between the two tendencies was never entirely resolved, the party eventually settled for the gradualist strategy and reached a substantial degree of unity in support of the devolution policy of the Labour government. In that phase, the party line was that, as its parliamentary leader put it, 'Scotland must be prepared to build on whatever devolution can be wrung out of this Government'.[7] This policy was maintained up to the referendum campaign in January–February 1979, when the SNP was indeed the only party to campaign unambiguously for a Yes vote. Despite the SNP's support for Labour's policy, at Westminster and in Scotland, the relations between the two parties remained frosty and led to them campaigning separately for the referendum. The SNP was fully aware that the hostility of the Labour party and the attacks of the No side were centred on the same nexus that was at the heart of the party's support for devolution: the connection with independence. Bearing that in mind, the party was very careful to avoid any linkage between the assembly and secession in its campaign for a Yes vote in the referendum. The paradoxical result was that, despite the hostility between the two parties, the SNP's pro-assembly discourse was virtually identical to Labour's. The tone of the SNP's campaign was well summarised by its deputy leader in the last week of the campaign when he based the party's case for devolution on three points.[8] First, Scottish distinctiveness as a historic nation hence its right to self-government. Secondly, the inefficiency and unaccountability of the status quo governing Scotland as Westminster had little time to devote to Scottish affairs and the political supervision of the Scottish Office was too limited. Thirdly, devolution being a matter of Scots showing confidence in themselves as a nation.

Perception and strategic use of the EU

In the 1970s, the SNP had a deeply negative perception of the European Union. The prevailing view was that European integration was the continuation, on a larger scale, of the process of political and economic centralisation that had taken place in the UK. As such, it threatened to inflict further damage on Scotland. In the party's eyes, the nature of European integration explained why the UK-wide parties were in favour of joining the EU. Billy Wolfe, the then leader, wrote in 1973 that 'it is the aim of the Common Market to establish political domination of the whole of Western Europe and to tolerate no deviation from this line'.[9] The SNP opposed entry into the EU in 1972 and campaigned for a No vote in the 1975 referendum. During the referendum campaign, the parliamentary leader of the party declared that the EU 'represents everything that our party has fought against: centralisation, undemocratic procedures, power politics and a fetish for abolishing cultural differences'.[10] The referendum itself was largely seen by the party as a referendum on Scottish sovereignty in the hope that Scotland would vote against the EU while England would vote in favour. After the majority of Scots had voted in favour of EU membership the party shifted its position towards acceptance of the reality of membership while keeping a negative attitude to the EU. In October 1978, the then deputy leader Gordon Wilson declared that 'a massive re-think by Scots about the EEC may be needed soon. Evidence is growing that the EEC is proving hostile to Scotland's national interests'.[11] The official party policy was that the issue of EU membership of an independent Scotland would be decided in a referendum with the SNP recommending withdrawal to the electorate.[12]

The party's hostility towards the EU was determined by three main factors. First, the SNP objected to Scotland not having been represented in the negotiations before entry and not having been consulted as a nation in the 1975 referendum. Closely connected with this aspect was the issue of Scotland's representation in the institutions of the EU and the preservation of its 'national' status vis-à-vis its categorisation as a 'region'. Second, most members of the SNP had a negative opinion of the political characteristics of the EU which was perceived as a centralising, bureaucratic and undemocratic organisation.[13] Third, the majority had a negative perception of the economic characteristics of the EU, in particular of its free-market nature and of the effects on Scotland of such policies as the Common Fisheries Policy.[14] From the party's perspective, the European Union was seen as adding an extra hurdle on the path towards achieving national sovereignty, hence secession from the UK but continued membership of the EU would achieve little. What Scotland urgently needed was secession from both the UK and the EU and the SNP policy in the 1970s aimed to achieve this double independence.

This perception determined that the European dimension was largely neglected in the SNP's campaign for a Yes vote in the 1979 referendum. In so far as the EU was mentioned, it was for pointing out its negative effects on Scotland. The declarations of two senior figures of the party, who would be at the forefront of the change of policy on the EU in the 1980s, during the campaign illustrate the point. The deputy leader Gordon Wilson failed to mention any European dimension within its case for devolution in the last stages of the referendum campaign[15] while Winnie Ewing declared that a No vote in the referendum would clear the way for 'the further takeover of Scottish land by foreigners . . . and for Brussels to dictate the final ruin of fishing and agriculture'.[16] In a defensive manner, the party thus played down the link between devolution and independence and did not exploit the European dimension to boost the latter's appeal.

The Labour party

Labour had long been – since 1959 – the first party in Scotland. In the October 1974 general election it obtained 36.3 per cent of votes and secured forty-one MPs. Five years later, at the May 1979 election, it increased its percentage of the vote to 41.5 per cent and gained forty-four seats.

Self-government policy

The Labour party, both at the British and Scottish levels, had long had a difficult relationship with the issue of Scottish self-government since its establishment at the end of the nineteenth century. The party had always been opposed to Scotland's secession from the UK but the question of devolved self-government presented difficulties. Scotland's distinctive identity and the demand for home rule were long-term features of Scottish politics and pre-dated the emergence of the party as the political voice of the labour movement. As self-government has always been closely associated with nationalist arguments and rhetoric, the relationship between the Labour party and Scottish self-government was largely shaped by the conflict between socialism and nationalism or, put another way, between class and territory. On the one hand, the party inherited the nineteenth century Liberal tradition of articulating the interests of the periphery vis-à-vis the centre and, in that light, support for devolution was a natural consequence of a more general positioning. On the other hand, the party espoused the socialist belief in internationalism and in centralised management of the economy. Both beliefs were clearly in conflict with a regional nationalism such as Scotland's. It is no coincidence that in the early twentieth century the party tended to be sympathetic towards self-government while it turned into opposition in the after-war period; a period during which the centrally planned welfare state reached its apogee. In 1958 it signalled its change of policy thus: 'Scotland's problems can best be solved by socialist planning on a UK scale'.[17]

Up to the late 1960s, however, the issue of Scotland's constitutional status was little more than a question of statements of principle. The rise of the SNP turned this into a salient political issue and, after the October 1974 election, setting up a Scottish assembly was the official policy of the Labour government. The policy took shape in two white papers, an abortive Scotland and Wales Bill 1976 and finally the Scotland Act 1978, which was put to the referendum in March 1979. The Act provided for the establishment of a Scottish assembly subject to approval in a referendum by at least 40 per cent of the Scottish electorate.

It is widely accepted in the literature that Labour's change of policy was a direct consequence of the electoral threat represented by the rise of the SNP. Given its relative weakness vis-à-vis the Conservatives in England, the party's chances of gaining office at the UK level were crucially affected by its performance in Scotland (and Wales).[18] However, if this was the vote-seeking rationale for the change of policy, Labour had to make it consistent with its overall ideological framework so as not to lose credibility. The leadership of the party did so on the basis of three main arguments, though these failed to unite the party behind the policy of devolution, as a sub-stantial section of the party, both at the UK and at the Scottish levels, remained opposed to devolution. First, that Scotland was a distinctive part of the United Kingdom and thus needed distinctive policies tailored to it, especially economic policies to redress its relative deprivation. Supporters of devolution on the left of the party stressed that self-government was neces-sary in order to adopt 'Scottish solutions to Scottish problems' and stem the economic decline of Scotland that was having a particularly harsh impact on the working class. Jim Sillars made the point succinctly by saying 'we cannot have socialism for Scotland without self-government'.[19] Secondly, that devolution was necessary to democratise the exercise of government in Scotland, which was in the hands of the bureaucrats in the Scottish Office. As Gordon Brown – then leader of the party's devolution committee – put it, 'now is the time to review a system where decisions are made not by politicians but by civil servants'.[20] The third, and more prosaic, argument was that devolution was necessary to placate Scots' legitimate desire for self-government and thus reject the attraction of the SNP's policy which was putting the unity of the UK at risk and, by so doing, jeopardising the interests of the Scottish working class. There was broad consensus that the traditional stance of the party in favour of the interests of the periphery and of furthering democracy – which had been overshadowed by economic issues in the 1950s and 1960s – needed to be re-emphasised to address the wave of increased identification with Scotland and of rising support for the SNP.[21] Not surprisingly, supporters of devolution pointed out that a large majority of Scots had consistently been in favour of a limited form of self-government and that only a small minority wanted Scotland to leave the UK. Support for the SNP had to be understood, among other reasons, as a reaction to the long-standing failure of the UK parties to deliver such constitutional reform. According to them, it followed that granting devolution to Scotland was very much likely to reduce support for the SNP and for independence rather than increase it.[22] The perception of the United Kingdom implicit in this discourse was threefold. First, the union between Scotland and England had been and still was beneficial for Scotland as a whole and for its working class in particular. Second, Scotland had economic, social and cultural specificities which warranted distinctive public policies carried out more democratically on a devolved basis without undermining the benefits of the union. Third, despite the discovery of North Sea oil, secession from the UK would be very damaging economically for Scotland besides being a selfish policy betraying solidarity between the Scottish and English working classes.

Opponents of devolution, on the other hand, used three arguments. First, that devolution could not provide economic powers sufficient to really make a difference to Scotland's economy, without threatening the economic and political advantages from centralised management of the economy on a UK basis. As the Scottish economy was highly integrated with the wider British economy, socialist policies to improve the condition of the Scottish working class could only be pursued on a UK-wide basis. Therefore, self-government was not in the interests of the Scottish working class and, by implication, should not be in the interests of the Labour party in Scotland. Second, that the advantages of devolution were more than outweighed by the disadvantage of losing influence in the UK government through a diminished role for the Secretary of State and a possible reduction in the number of MPs, which would threaten the territorial redistribution of resources in Scotland's favour.[23] Third, but most importantly, a substantial minority led by Tam Dalyell, MP for the then constituency of West Lothian, was strongly opposed to devolution because they saw it as the first step in the process of breaking up the United Kingdom. As Dalyell put it: 'there was an authentic section of the Labour Party which believed that devolution would lead to separation'.[24] In sum, a substantial section of the party considered the assembly not to have enough constitutional powers to have a significant impact on the issues that mattered most to the Scottish working class and, on the other hand, to pose a very serious threat to the union between Scotland and England.

Given this sharp conflict of opinions, the party was never able to unite behind the official government policy. The divisions within the party were both vertical and horizontal. On the one hand, the devolution policy always maintained its original nature of a distinctly 'elite' project, elaborated by the party leadership in London and somewhat imposed on the rest of the party. On the other hand, once a Scottish assembly became a concrete prospect, the pro-devolution wing of the Scottish party started to demand a more vigorous form of devolution than the 'London' party could concede, especially with regard to economic and fiscal powers.[25] Indeed, in December 1975 a group of devolutionists led by Jim Sillars left the party on the ground that the leadership had betrayed Scotland's hopes and set up a rival Scottish Labour party with a more radical devolutionist agenda.[26]

These divisions became implacably exposed by the party's inability to conduct a unified campaign for the 1979 referendum. It split into three main groups with most of the party joining the official *Labour Movement Yes Campaign* and others taking part in the *Yes for Scotland* and the *Labour Vote No* campaign. At the core of the matter, there was the link between devolution and secession. This was the main motive behind the *Labour Vote No* group fronted by Tam Dalyell and it was the force keeping Labour and the SNP apart. In a newspaper article published during the referendum campaign, Dalyell wrote: 'a Yes would put us firmly on a motorway without exit, with a destination of separation from England – a journey on which the majority of Labour activists do not wish to travel . . . March 1 is indeed our last chance – to cry halt to this juggernaut which could break-up Britain'.[27] The leadership of the party in Scotland ruled out conducting a joint campaign with the SNP on the ground that that would constitute, in the words of the then secretary Helen Liddell, 'soiling our hands'.[28] The party even rejected a single Yes-side broadcast during the campaign because it would have meant sharing it with the SNP.[29] Indeed, the party went beyond merely keeping its distance from the SNP, it explicitly directed its pro-devolution discourse against nationalism and independence and presented its policy as the best antidote to SNP's separatism. The Chancellor of the Exchequer, Denis Healey, in a speech in Glasgow six days before the referendum, was at pains to emphasise that an assembly would not be 'a staging post to independence', that 'Scotland does not want independence. But Scots do want a greater say over their own affairs' and that 'the Labour party is not afraid of Scottish nationalism and separatism. We have tackled it head on at recent by-elections and given it a thrashink [sic]'.[30] The referendum campaign thus dramatically exposed the conflict between principles and rational calculations of benefits and costs of constitutional change which lay at the heart of Labour's policy.

Perception and strategic use of the EU

The issue of accession to the European Union was profoundly divisive for the Labour party throughout the 1970s and the party's dominant attitude was one of hostility. At the time of the UK negotiation and ratification of the decision to join the EU in 1971–73, the majority of the Labour party was against both the idea of membership in itself and the terms negotiated by the Conservative government. During the campaign for the June 1975 referendum the Labour leadership did not officially take sides and left members, even at ministerial level, free to campaign for or against membership but the grassroots were largely opposed to membership.[31] After the referendum result, the party accepted the reality of EU membership but maintained a predominantly negative attitude. The roots of this attitude were in the perception of the EU as a capitalist organisation, both in political and economic terms, and in the constraints the EU put on the pursuit of socialist policies in the UK.[32]

The Scottish party broadly shared the attitude of the UK party but also expressed specific concerns related to the impact of EU membership on Scotland and on the question of Scottish self-government. These concerns were both economic and political. With regard to the former, Scottish Labour feared that Scotland would be at an economic disadvantage within the EU. As Jim Sillars and others put it, 'having long experience of the inherent difficulties of economic and social life on the periphery of one common market (Britain), Scots were not keen on becoming even more peripheral in the larger European common market'.[33] Scotland would thus suffer economic costs because its peripherality would be exacerbated by the larger size of the European market and it would be compounded by the capitalist character of the EU. The political concerns were related to two issues. First, the fact that entry into the EU had been negotiated by a Conservative government with minority support in Scotland and that the Scottish people had not been consulted on the issue. If this problem was solved by the Scottish popular vote in favour of membership in the 1975 referendum, the second one was still on the table. Namely, whether Scottish interests were adequately represented at the EU level.[34]

Some leading Scottish pro-devolutionists, notably Jim Sillars and, to a lesser extent, John Mackintosh, made an explicit connection between membership of the EU, the prospect of further integration on the European scale and Scottish self-government, arguing that the former two strengthened the case for the latter. Referring to the prospect of EU membership, Sillars stated as early as 1972 that 'in the changing circumstances of today and tomorrow it will become much more difficult to hold the Union together'.[35] In his semi-autobiography, he also wrote 'there was the question of the EEC, with British entry, in my view, pushing Scotland further away from the influential centres of decision-making'.[36] The 1974 pamphlet on devolution he co-authored, reckoned that 'if Britain remains within the EEC we foresee further problems for Scotland and for her relationship with the rest of the UK'.[37] This was due to two reasons. First, the 'forced entry to the EEC' had resulted in a 'greater stimulus to national feeling'.[38] Second, because 'devolution within a Britain sovereign and independent is one thing, but we suggest that the coming years will show that is not the same as devolution within a Britain increasingly becoming an integral part of the Common Market, with all that implies about the transfer of power from Westminster to Brussels'.[39] In a debate in the Commons in 1975, Sillars said:

> if we are locked inside the EEC I would not argue that Scotland should come out . . . but I would certainly argue that it would then be in the interests of the Scottish people to have direct nation-State membership of the Community. If we were foolish enough to continue inside the EEC it might be time to write a new verse to an old song.[40]

Jim Sillars went even further when he left the Labour party to found the breakaway Scottish Labour party, declaring that 'the European dimension *requires* Scottish autonomy'[41] because

> without a Scottish Assembly with powers in the industrial field Scotland would be unable to withstand the dual centralist pressures of the United Kingdom and EEC . . . Our Scotland lies on the periphery of industrial Europe and the disadvantage we suffer in the market place can only be balanced with the political weight of an Assembly which had power to pursue policies suited to our scale and abilities.[42]

John Mackintosh, the most consistent post-war supporter of devolution, thought that membership of the EU would weaken the sense of identification with Britain, 'the Scots may come to look to Brussels more than to London for those aspects of policy that are clearly outside the control of Scotland'.[43] He also acknowledged the central question of the representation of Scottish interests at the EU level and advocated a separate Scottish representation within the British delegation as the logical consequence of devolution.[44]

In their statements, Sillars and Mackintosh, and those who shared their views, were identifying three main connections between integration at the European level and self-government in Scotland. First, that participation in the process of European integration would weaken Scots' identification with the UK and raise nationalist demands. Second, that Scotland was in a disadvantaged position within the EU both in economic terms, being on the periphery of the large European market, and in political terms, its interests not being adequately represented in Brussels, the new political centre. As a consequence, participation in the process of European integration was making the need for a devolved self-government in Scotland stronger in order to soften the negative impact of EU membership on Scotland and to dampen secessionist demands.

Many elements of the debate on European integration and Scottish self-government which would become widespread in the 1990s were thus already present in the 1970s. However, both Sillars and Mackintosh were visionary, maverick politicians with limited party following and their views did not have significant influence in the party. Sillars's decision to leave Labour and to establish the Scottish Labour party clearly illustrates the point. Beyond matters of personality and vision, the fundamental difference between Sillars and Mackintosh on the one hand and the bulk of the party on the other hand was that the former were convinced that Scotland's disadvantaged position within the European common market required more government competences at the Scottish level while the latter thought that, on the contrary, only government action at the UK level could soften the EU's negative impact on Scotland. To many Labour members, notably those sceptical of or hostile to devolution, the prospect of European integration was weakening rather than strengthening the case for self-government.[45] To those in favour of devolution, the European dimension appeared largely uninfluential, not least because it was mentally associated with foreign policy, a competence that would not be devolved to the proposed assembly.

Partly because of this conflict of interpretations and partly because Labour's devolution policy in the late 1970s was in essence more an exercise of damage limitation against the electoral threat of the SNP than one of creative thinking, the connection between European integration and Scottish self-government remained confined to the intellectual debate and had little influence on the party's policy. During the campaign for the 1979 referendum, the European dimension was notably absent from Labour's rhetoric.[46]

The Conservative party

The Conservative party was the traditional second party in Scotland. It won 24.7 per cent of the vote and sixteen seats in October 1974 and increased these to 31.4 per cent and twenty-two seats in 1979.

Self-government policy

In a similar way to the Labour party, the Conservative party had also had a difficult relationship with the issue of Scotland's constitutional status. The Scottish section of the party was called the Scottish Unionist party during the period 1912–65 and the party had always had a fundamental belief in the union between Scotland and England and therefore in the preservation of the United Kingdom.[47] Any constitutional reform with the potential to endanger the integrity of the UK was naturally opposed by the party. This obviously included independence but also, on the ground of the connection discussed above, home rule.

This unionism rested on four key beliefs about the United Kingdom. First, the party did not deny Scotland's distinctiveness from England. On the contrary the British union was conceptualised as the union of two nations in the form of a union-state whose function was precisely to preserve the distinctiveness of the Scottish nation. Nonetheless, second, the party perceived the UK as more than simply a pluri-national state. It can be said that it perceived it as a two-level national state, in which a Scottish nation (and an English one) co-existed within a wider British nation. Primary national identification among Conservatives was with the UK as a whole rather than with Scotland. Third, the party perceived the historical experience of the union with England as a particularly successful one for Scotland which had gained enormously both politically and economically. That perception was true for the past and remained true for the 1970s. Last, but not least, the party thought that the constitutional status quo – with over-representation in the House of Commons, direct representation in the Cabinet and favourable financial transfers – was the one best able to maximise Scotland's interests within the United Kingdom.

Despite this long-held commitment to unionism and opposition to home rule, the party supported the establishment of an assembly in the period 1968–76, though in a vague and non-committal fashion.[48] After 1976, under the new Thatcher leadership, the Conservatives adopted a two-pronged strategy. On the one hand, they continued to support the principle of devolved self-government for Scotland in declarations and conference motions, though without defining the exact type of devolution envisaged. On the other hand, they opposed the government's policy on the ground that it represented a flawed model and the large majority of the parliamentary party voted against the Scotland and Wales Bill 1976 and the Scotland Bill 1977.[49] This has to be seen in the context created by the official presentation of the Scotland and Wales Bill with which devolution ceased to be a Scottish issue with a low UK profile and became one of the main policies of the Labour government. After 1976, devolution became a major partisan issue and, by implication, opposition to the government bills became an important tactical weapon in the competition between the two parties. If in the earlier phase the Scottish Conservative support for devolution was intended as a competitive weapon against the SNP, after 1976 the party decided to compete primarily against Labour rather than the SNP. In May 1978 the Scottish party decided to 'campaign vigorously for a No vote in the referendum'[50] and with some minor defections the party teamed up with the business organisations in the *Scotland Says No* group to fight against the assembly in the 1979 referendum.

On the basis of this two-pronged strategy, the party campaigned on a clear distinction between the principle of devolution and the Scotland Act 1978. It made it clear that by no means did opposition to the Scotland Act mean opposition to devolution and it hinted that a future Conservative government would enact a sounder devolution policy. This was expressed most clearly in the interventions of Margaret Thatcher and, especially, Lord Home – a former prime minister and hitherto prominent devolutionist – calling for a No vote in the referendum.[51] With that distinction emphasised, the party turned its attacks against the Act and concentrated on three aspects. First, it claimed that the assembly would add an extra layer of government and bureaucracy without having the necessary competences, in particular fiscal powers, to meet the expectations of the Scottish electorate. Secondly, it stressed that the assembly was likely to be dominated by Labour given that it would have been elected by the first-past-the-post system and that the Conservative party was already in decline in Scotland. Lastly, but most importantly, it warned that the likely conflicts between the assembly and Westminster would be exploited by the SNP to fuel support for secession and that, therefore, devolution would likely lead to the break-up of the UK. Indeed, in the months between the assent to the Scotland Act and the referendum, the party increasingly focused its discourse on the issue of the break-up of the UK. The Conservative party spokesman on devolution, Leon (now Lord) Brittan emphasised during the campaign his 'fears of a Scotland separated from the rest of Britain'.[52] Thatcher herself warned that the assembly would 'institutionalise conflict between Westminster and Edinburgh. That conflict threatens the very survival of the United Kingdom. Scotland on Thursday decides the future of many more people than her own. I believe that the Scottish people will reaffirm their belief in the United Kingdom so that we may all continue our journey together'.[53]

Even though the tactic of warning that the assembly would lead to secession while at the same time still endorsing the principle of devolution appeared to its opponents to have little credibility,[54] the combined effect of the No campaign was ultimately successful in turning a large enough section

of the electorate against the assembly in the referendum. This was the effect
the Shadow Secretary of State, Teddy Taylor, claimed was under way almost
one month before the referendum, when he stated:

> the tide was turning in the referendum debate and that Scots were now beginning
> to realise that what had originally appeared as a scheme to help Scotland was not
> so . . . devolution would simply be a costly and bureaucratic extra tier of govern-
> ment which would create frustration and lay the seeds for the break-up of the UK.[55]

Perception and strategic use of the EU

In the 1970s, the Conservatives were perceived to be the party of 'Europe'
since it was they who took the UK into the European Union in 1973, who
subsequently made the greatest contribution to the Yes campaign in the 1975
referendum and who were, in comparison with the other parties (except the
Liberals), the most pro-EU. On the European issue, the Scottish party was
very much in the same position as the UK party; Scottish Conservatives were
largely in favour of EU membership and tended to take a British rather than
a purely Scottish view.[56] The party's support for the EU was essentially based
on the expected economic benefits to be derived from membership of a
customs union in line with the Conservative belief in free trade and economic
internationalisation, which, in the eyes of the party, outweighed the negative
political aspects.[57] These were mainly related to the potential threats the EU
represented to the notion of sovereignty of the UK Parliament and to the links
between Britain and the Commonwealth. Overall, the economic aspects of
EU membership were thought to be much more salient than the political ones
and, accordingly, the EU was perceived by the party as an essentially economic
organisation.

The Conservatives thought that membership of the EU and the prospect
of direct elections to the European Parliament ran counter the demand
for Scottish self-government because they exacerbated the risk of 'over-
government' for Scotland. The Shadow Secretary of State, pointing out that
with the creation of an assembly there would be European MPs, Westminster
MPs and Assembly MPs said 'The Three Parliaments will all be making laws
and regulations and there's a real danger of Scotland becoming the most over-
governed country in the world'.[58] Most of them also thought that entry into
the EU limited the range of competences that could be devolved to a Scottish
assembly and that the movement towards integration on a continental scale
undermined the very principle of devolution.[59] Overall, though, the dominant perception within the party was that the EU dimension was not relevant
for the question of Scotland's self-government, the two issues being largely
seen as not connected.

For these reasons, the issues of European integration and of Scottish self-government remained largely independent from each other in the policy of the Conservative party in the 1970s and membership of the EU appears as having had close to no influence on the party's policy.[60] Where a link between these two issues existed it was more because they touched upon the same question, e.g. parliamentary sovereignty, than because the European dimension affected the perception of devolution within the UK.

Conclusions

The rise of the SNP, a party whose raison d'être was to radically change Scotland's constitutional status, made self-government a salient political issue and an object of party competition. It did so because its success threatened the position of the two main UK-wide parties – especially Labour – and thus forced them to respond by addressing the policy issue at the heart of the competitive challenge. As the parties developed their responses, they moved to occupy three points on the policy space in correspondence with the three main constitutional options, with the SNP associated with independence, Labour with devolution and the Conservatives with the status quo. This structured the politics of self-government along party lines and was a far cry from the pre-1974 period when Scottish self-government was not a matter of political cleavage and the policies of the two main parties were both vague and broadly similar. However, this process of polarisation was still incomplete, as demonstrated by the divisions in the Labour party and by the ambiguous Conservative position of opposing the Scotland Act 1978 while still supporting the principle of devolution.

The European Union was perceived in negative terms by the SNP and by Labour and in positive terms by the Conservatives. The analysis of the determinants of this variance indicates that ideological attitudes to free trade and capitalist market competition were the key factors. This pattern of attitudes towards the EU meant that a negative perception of the EU was associated with the demand for self-government while opposition to the latter was associated with a pro-EU position. The common element was that all three parties perceived few connections between the European dimension and Scotland's constitutional status and therefore saw the former as of little relevance for the latter. This led to the decision not to use the European dimension in their respective strategies pro- and anti-devolution in the campaign for the 1979 referendum. Positive use of the European dimension by Labour and the SNP was virtually ruled out by the hostility of the two parties towards the EU and the 'negative' argument that the threat of European integration strengthened the case for self-government was too abstract and too elitist to be of practical use. On the contrary, the argument that devolution in addition to its many problems also ran counter to the historical trend towards European integration and economic internationalisation was more effective.

As a result of the exclusion of the European dimension, competition between parties in the 1979 campaign was played within an exclusively UK dimension in which the pro-self-government parties – Labour and the SNP – were at a structural disadvantage versus their opponents. At the roots of this disadvantage lay the link between devolution and independence and widespread hostility towards the latter. The SNP was forced to play down the link at the risk of making its rhetoric virtually indistinguishable from Labour's while the latter was trapped in the contradiction of advocating devolution as an antidote to secession while the dominant perception was that it was rather a stepping-stone to it. As Perman remarked, 'there was an obvious contradiction between Labour urging a "Yes" vote against separation and the SNP urging a "Yes" vote as a means to independence'.[61] This produced the remarkable result that Labour No campaigners were less hostile vis-à-vis Conservative Yes campaigners than Labour Yes campaigners were vis-à-vis Nationalists, i.e. that conflict intensity was actually higher within the Yes campaign than between the latter and the No campaign.[62] Inevitably, this fatally weakened the Yes side both organisationally – through the fragmentation of the Yes campaign – and presentationally – by making it much more difficult to put across the Yes argument. It is thus not surprising that the conflicts and the contradictions within the Yes campaign have long been seen as a decisive element in the failure of the Yes side to obtain enough support in the referendum. This situation was exploited to the full by the Conservative party and the business organisations which could count on a less fragmented No campaign organisation and, more importantly, on a more coherent No argument. By centring their strategy on the links between devolution and independence, the Conservatives and their allies exploited the divisions and the contradictions among their opponents and, through their influence on public opinion, defeated the latter's policy in the referendum.[63] More generally, a 'British' camp of Conservative and Labour anti-devolutionists defeated a 'Scottish' camp of Nationalists and Labour pro-devolutionists.

Notes

1 On the Scottish party system in general, see, among others, Bennie et al. (1997).
2 See Dardanelli (2002: 70).
3 See Bennie et al. (1997: 81–2).

4 See Levy (1986) and Kauppi (1982).

5 Macartney (1981: 18).

6 On the conflict within the party on devolution before and after the referendum, see Kauppi (1982: 333–4).

7 Quoted in Mbadinuju (1976: 296).

8 Gordon Wilson, 'Assembly Would Give Better Value for Taxpayers' Money'. *The Courier and Advertiser*, 26 February 1979.

9 Wolfe (1973: 139).

10 Quoted in Lynch (1996: 35).

11 Scottish National party archive, Acc 10754/27.

12 *Choose Scotland – The Challenge of Independence*, p. 11.

13 Wolfe and Wilson, interviews with the author; see also press releases by Gordon Wilson, Douglas Henderson, George Reid, Hamish Watt and Winnie Ewing between 21 October 1978 and 28 February 1979 in Scottish National Party Archive, Acc 10754/27.

14 Wilson, interview with the author.

15 Wilson, 'Assembly Would Give Better Value for Taxpayers' Money'.

16 As reported in 'Yes Vote Would Be Sign of Confidence', *The Scotsman*, 7 February 1979.

17 Quoted in Mitchell (1996: 312); see also Keating and Bleiman (1979: 146–7).

18 On Labour being dependent on the Scottish seats, see, among others, Bennie et al. (1997: 46). For evidence of the devolution policy being directed against the SNP, see *Scotland Will Win with Labour*, pp. 8 and 16–17.

19 Reported in Sillars (1986: 75).

20 Quoted in 'Time to Make Decisions "Accountable" ', *The Scotsman*, 15 February 1979.

21 See Keating and Bleiman (1979: 178).

22 This was despite the fact that vote for the SNP did not imply support for independence, see Miller et al. (1977).

23 See, among others, Keating and Bleiman (1979: 176) and Bogdanor (1999: 173).

24 Quoted in Miller (1980: 113); see also Dalyell (1977).

25 See Keating and Bleiman (1979: especially 179) and Wood (1981: especially 122).

26 See Drucker (1978) and Sillars (1986: 55–80).

27 Tam Dalyell, 'Your Last Chance to Stop this Juggernaut'. *Glasgow Herald*, 15 February 1979.

28 Quoted in Macartney (1981: 17).

29 See 'Referendum Debate', *The Scotsman*, 17 February 1979.

30 'Assembly not Staging Post, says Healey', *Glasgow Herald*, 23 February 1979.

31 See Byrd (1978: 145–6).

32 See *The Better Way for Scotland*, pp. 24–5; see also Byrd (1978: 130–4) and Daniels (1998: 74).

33 Eadie et al. (1974: 7).

34 Ibidem: 11. Millan, interview with the author, acknowledges the economic factors but reckons that political and historical factors were much more important.

35 Quoted in Eadie et al. (1974: 7).

36 Sillars (1986: 36).

37 Eadie et al. (1974: 11).

38 Ibidem: 7.

39 Ibidem: 11.
40 Sillars (1986: 61).
41 Ibidem: 62; italics in original.
42 Sillars (1986: 59).
43 Mackintosh (1982: 202).
44 Ibidem: 203.
45 Though some, such as Dalyell (1977: 49–51), were aware that the EU had the potential to facilitate the case for self-government.
46 See Bochel et al. (1981: especially 180–91).
47 On the component elements of the Unionist ideology, see Mitchell (1990: 8–14).
48 On the different forms of devolution the party supported between 1968 and 1976, see Mitchell (1990: 52–83).
49 See Mitchell (1990: 74–5).
50 Ibidem: 88.
51 See 'No Vote Will not Kill Devolution, Pledges Thatcher', *Glasgow Herald*, 28 February 1979 and 'Lord Home Rejects "Last Chance" claim', *The Scotsman*, 15 February 1979.
52 Quoted in 'Labour Claim is Blackmail, Says Brittan', *The Scotsman*, 19 February 1979.
53 'No Vote Will not Kill Devolution, Pledges Thatcher'.
54 See Mitchell (1990: 89).
55 ' "Yes the No's Are Winning", Says Taylor', *Glasgow Herald*, 6 February 1979.
56 Hutton and Rifkind, interviews with the author.
57 See Ashford (1980: 112) and Morris (1996: 130); for a specifically Scottish perspective, see Dalziel (1980: especially 232) and Hutton, interview with the author.
58 ' "Conservatives Care Little for Scotland", says Reid', *The Scotsman*, 3 February 1979; see also ' "Recipe for Chaos", say Tories', *The Scotsman*, 9 February 1979.
59 See Greenwood and Wilson (1978).
60 See, for instance, the *Conservative Manifesto for Scotland* 1979, p. 24.
61 Perman (1979: 56).
62 See Perman (1979: 55–7) and Aitken (1997: 258).
63 On the impact of Conservative rhetoric focused on the threat of a break-up of the UK, see 'Tories Could Hold the Key to Vote on 1 March', *The Scotsman*, 19 February 1979.

3
Interest groups

Interest groups were the other key elite actors who played a crucial role in the politics of self-government. Some of them had a historical presence within Scottish society and/or a large membership which lent them a degree of representativeness in 'interpreting' public opinion and in turn to shape it even superior to that of political parties. The key groups analysed here are the Church of Scotland, the Scottish Trades Union Congress (STUC) and the business organisations. Following the pattern of chapter 2, for each of these actors I analyse their policy on self-government, the perception they had of the European Union – in general and in relation to their position on Scottish self-government in particular – and whether they used the European dimension in their strategies.

What emerges from the analysis is that each of the three interest groups had a different pattern of attitudes towards the EU and devolution. The Church of Scotland and business organisations were pro-EU while the STUC was hostile whereas the latter and the Church supported devolution while business was opposed. The Church of Scotland was thus the only group who had a positive attitude to both. This led to the Church seeing positive connections between the two and exploiting them in its pro-self-government discourse. In contrast the STUC and the business organisations perceived the EU dimensions as running counter to the demands for self-government or at best being irrelevant to it. In a similar fashion to the pattern observed among political parties, thus, the prevailing pattern was of a negative association between demand for self-government and support for the EU and the failure to exploit the European dimension either to strengthen or to weaken the case for devolution.

The Church of Scotland

The Church of Scotland is one of the national institutions that have preserved Scottish distinctiveness within the United Kingdom throughout the years.

It still had a large membership in the 1970s and its General Assembly had often been perceived as a proxy for a Scottish Parliament.[1] By virtue of its national status and its large membership, the Church had always considered its right and duty to take a position on political affairs as an interpreter and a representative of public opinion.[2] In order to effectively take part in social and political debates, the Church had set up in 1919 a Church and Nation committee charged with monitoring political developments and advising the General Assembly on what actions the Church might take. It is mainly through the work of this committee that the Church took part in the debate on Scotland's constitutional status.[3]

Self-government policy

The Church of Scotland had long been sympathetic to the idea of Scottish self-government. Since the 1968 General Assembly, the official position of the Church was to support 'an effective form of self-government within the framework of the United Kingdom',[4] though there were internal divisions, especially between the Church and Nation committee and the wider membership. The former was consistently more pro-devolution than the Church as a whole while many members, especially those close to the Conservative party, were hostile. In the period 1974–79, the Church was in favour of establishing an assembly with substantial economic and fiscal powers, elected on the basis of a system of proportional representation.[5] Hence, the Church supported the devolution policy of the Labour government though it was critical of the failure to adopt a system of proportional representation and of the powers conferred on an assembly, especially in the initial proposals of the *Our Changing Democracy* white paper and of the Scotland and Wales Bill 1976.

The Church was also at pains to stress that it supported devolution as a viable and desirable constitutional status in its own right and that it opposed independence.[6] However, its opposition to secession did not display the hostility of the other interest groups, as discussed below, and its discourse on self-government had clear nationalist overtones, at times reminiscent of the SNP's. This perspective transpires from the Church's attitudes towards the union between Scotland and England and its willingness to accept independence as an acceptable option, albeit not a desirable one. The British Union was often referred to in critical language and the establishment of a Scottish assembly as 'the restoration of a Scottish legislature' thus making an explicit link with the pre-1707 Parliament.[7] Both a negative interpretation of the Union with England and the interpretation of self-government as re-establishing what was 'stolen' in 1707 were central features of the Nationalist discourse on self-government.[8] The attitude towards independence was shown in the aftermath of the fall of the Scotland and Wales devolution bill in February 1977 amid concerns that plans for devolution would be shelved. The Church reacted by advocating holding a multi-choice referendum with options ranging from the status quo to independence to give Scots 'an opportunity to indicate the degree of self-government that they wanted'.[9] By supporting the idea of a multi-option referendum, the Church was thus legitimising the secession option.

Although the reports of the Church and Nation committee did not explicitly spell it out, the Church's support for self-government in the 1970s appears to have been determined by three factors. At a general level, it was the desire to defend Scottish interests, particularly those which were supposed to be safeguarded by the Treaty of Union and to enhance Scotland's autonomy within the UK. Secondly, it was the desire to democratise the way Scotland was governed and to make it more responsive to citizens' needs. Underlying the other factors, however, it was probably also the desire to enhance the Church's influence within Scottish society on the ground that this would have been easier to do with a devolved assembly than under the constitutional status quo.[10]

The Church's position on devolution and independence and, especially, the connection between the two self-government options became salient issues during the referendum campaign. Although the official position of the Church remained consistently in favour of devolution throughout the 1974–79 period, the sizeable minority who were hostile became increasingly vocal. The minority argued that there was no single Christian interpretation of Scottish self-government, hence the Church's position was unacceptably partisan. The conflict between the official position and the dissenting minority surfaced dramatically during the campaign. The Church and Nation committee prepared a statement to be read in all churches on the two Sundays before the referendum calling for a Yes vote, expecting that the statement would be endorsed by the General Assembly. However, the statement was challenged and successfully blocked by the critical minority with the paradoxical result that, despite its long-standing support for devolution, the Church's position on the referendum was formally neutral.[11]

The evidence shows that the rebels' leader was primarily motivated by the fear of secession. In a newspaper article published during the referendum campaign, he wrote:

> The Yes man has been convinced we can stop at an assembly. He says he wants devolution but not separation. If that's his position the sooner he becomes a No man the better . . . one thing is certain it is that the proposed Act will just not work and when the inevitable disillusion sets in the hard-liners will come around with their demand that we go the whole way – nothing else will get us what we deserve. And by that time they'll have an attentive audience.[12]

Ten years after the referendum, he reaffirmed the same position, stating: 'for myself I have no time for the idea of separation and took a fairly active part on the "No" side at the time of the National Referendum'.[13]

Perception and strategic use of the EU

In the early 1970s the Church of Scotland was divided on the issue of membership of the EU with its General Assembly mainly opposed to UK's entry. In the run-up to the June 1975 referendum, however, the Church did not take a clear position but its opinion seemed to lean towards a Yes vote.[14] After the referendum, the Church adopted an increasingly positive attitude towards the EU and by the end of the decade its position was more supportive of the EU than that of most of Scottish society, as exemplified by its support for the direct election of the European Parliament, seen as a bold exercise of franchise beyond the state level and a welcome step towards the democratisation of the EU.[15]

The Church's positive attitude towards the EU appears to have been determined by four main factors, related to both the perception of the EU itself and of its impact on Scotland. At a general level, the Church was sympathetic towards European integration because it saw it as a process based on a healthy spirit of reconciliation and co-operation among the European countries after centuries of rivalry and war.[16] In terms of the direct relevance for Scotland, the Church emphasised three main points. First of all, the Church reckoned that the question of membership had been definitively settled by the 1975 referendum and that the option of withdrawal, apart from being fraught with practical problems, appeared to be against the tide of history. As a report of the Church and Nation committee put it, 'in a world which is becoming increasingly interdependent, it is hard to escape the conclusion that the most hopeful future for Scotland must be in a European setting'.[17] Secondly, the Church argued that Scotland's place was in Europe not only in view of the future but also on the basis of the past, in which the links between Scotland and continental Europe were particularly strong. A few years after the 1979 referendum, it even asserted, 'the traditional links between Scotland and the Continent in the Reformed Church, the Law, the Universities and much of our trade have been even closer than with England'.[18] Last, but by no means least, the Church believed that EU membership was benefiting Scotland's economic interests and that the problems that existed with EU policies such as agriculture and fisheries, though real, could be resolved.[19]

The Church of Scotland utilised the European dimension in its discourse pro-self-government in two main ways. Firstly, the Church claimed that the UK's participation in the EU strengthened the case for self-government for

Scotland, on the grounds that allowing full expression of diversity within the UK would have placed the latter in line with most other countries in Europe and would have allowed it to play its full part in Europe.[20] This was an attempt to legitimise Scottish self-government by claiming that it was in line with the process of integration and with the constitutional structure of many other European countries. Secondly, but most importantly, the Church exploited the issue of Scotland's representation at the Union level to argue that it was inadequate under the constitutional status quo and that, therefore, UK membership of the EU was adding extra urgency to the need for a devolved government. In its reports to the General Assembly, the Church and Nation committee pointed out that a specific Scottish representation was difficult to envisage under the constitutional status quo and explicitly considered devolution as a way of rectifying the problem.[21] The Church and Nation committee's reports repeatedly demanded that the proposed Scottish assembly be endowed with significant powers of representation at the Union level.[22]

The analysis of the Church of Scotland's attitude towards the EU and of its use of the European dimension thus shows that the Church perceived the European Union as offering Scottish actors both further incentives to demand self-government – in order to rectify the lack of adequate representation of Scottish interests at the Union level – and the opportunity to increase the legitimacy of their demand – by linking it to a 'progressive' development. The Church exploited these incentives and opportunities in its discourse in favour of self-government.

The Scottish Trades Union Congress

The Scottish Trades Union Congress (STUC) was the umbrella organisation of the Scottish trades union movement. Though most large trade unions were members of both the STUC and the British TUC, many small unions with an overwhelmingly Scottish membership were only affiliated with the STUC. The STUC was thus the voice of the Scottish working class and in this capacity it performed the role of both a 'class' and a 'national' organisation. Its class dimension also enabled it to speak for that section of Scottish society that was unrepresented by the traditional institutions of the Church, the legal and educational systems, which were essentially middle-class in character.[23] The STUC had always been close to the Labour party but in the 1970s it was also strongly influenced by the Communist party.[24] Its role of representative of the Scottish working class and of unofficial 'voice of Scotland' was particularly in evidence in the period 1974–79 as a result of the general closeness between the trade unions and the Labour government.[25]

The STUC operated through two main policy-making bodies: the General Council and the annual Congress. The General Council acted as the permanent secretariat and its staff was representing the trades union movement as a whole rather than the individual unions. It was the public face of the STUC and was charged with carrying out the STUC's policies. The main decision-making body was the annual Congress, in which all the unions affiliated to the STUC were taking part and at which policy decisions in the form of motions carried or rejected were taken. The sources analysed here are the reports of the STUC Annual Congress.

Self-government policy

Since its establishment at the end of the nineteenth century, the STUC had always been favourable to Scottish home rule in principle. From the 1969 Congress onwards, it became a formal policy objective.[26] Over the period 1974–79, the STUC advocated the establishment of a Scottish assembly with significant economic and fiscal powers. In particular, the STUC wanted the Scottish assembly to have control over the Scottish Development Agency (SDA) and the power to vary the rate of income tax, in addition to responsibility for the Scottish legal system, Scottish universities, agriculture and fisheries. However, the STUC wanted to retain equal conditions for Scottish workers and therefore was anxious to make sure labour legislation would not be devolved to the assembly and did not support the adoption of proportional representation for the assembly elections, as long as Westminster elections were still held under the plurality system.[27] The STUC was thus supportive of the Labour government's devolution policy in principle but it was critical of the government's initial proposals contained in the *Our Changing Democracy* white paper and in the Scotland and Wales Bill 1976.[28] As the Scotland Act 1978 moved closer to its position, the STUC strengthened its support for the government's policy. However, it was strongly opposed to holding a referendum – especially with the 40 per cent clause – and denounced it as a delaying tactic devised by the anti-devolutionists.[29] In the end the STUC joined the Scottish Labour party in the *Labour Movement Yes Campaign*, the main campaign group on the Yes side.[30] Throughout the period, the STUC continued to be very strongly opposed to secession and was deeply hostile towards the SNP.[31] The STUC was at pains to explain that by no means was support for devolution to be understood as covert support for independence and that, on the contrary, devolving power to Scottish institutions in the framework of the UK was the best antidote to the appeal of the SNP's policy. During the referendum campaign, its leader stated that 'failure to achieve an Assembly will put Scotland on the "slippery slope to separation"'.[32]

The STUC's support for self-government appears to have been determined by three main factors. The first one was a concern with Scotland's economic decline and its relative deprivation vis-à-vis other regions of the United Kingdom. The STUC believed that this could be effectively tackled only by governmental action at the Scottish level, though within the UK framework. As John Boyd, one of the leaders, put it in the mid-1970s: 'I am slowly and painfully coming to the conclusion that the only answer to Scotland's economic problem is Scottish government'.[33] The economic motive was explicit in a resolution adopted at the 1975 congress stating that 'the demand for a Scottish Assembly arises from continued economic deprivation and high unemployment, and a genuine desire among the Scottish people for a greater control of their own affairs'.[34] For this reason, the STUC was committed to 'meaningful devolution and to the establishment of a Scottish Assembly having the power and ability to influence the economic, political and social decision-making process in Scotland'[35], hence its emphasis on economic powers.

The economic aspect was closely linked to the second factor, namely the desire to enhance the democratic accountability of the Scottish Office. The issue had long figured in the Congress's discourse and was prominently on display in its campaign for an assembly. As the then secretary, Jimmy Milne, put it, 'it should bring the decision-making process closer to the people of Scotland . . . It will be an improvement in the democratic process, as decisions which are to be applied in Scotland will be made in Scotland'.[36]

It should come as no surprise, thirdly, that the theme of democratisation was also linked to the STUC's interest in strengthening its influence on public policy and to wider ideological considerations. As the STUC did not have direct access to the UK Labour party and to Westminster and the higher profile it enjoyed in the secondhalf of the 1970s was more an exception than the norm, its ability to influence UK public policy was limited. Autonomous legislative and governmental capabilities at the Scottish level would have undoubtedly increased the STUC's ability to influence public policy.[37] It also had clear ideological connotations. As mentioned above, the STUC was politically to the left of the Labour party as it was strongly influenced by communist ideas. Since Scotland had already in the 1970s a clear left-wing bias relative to the rest of the UK, it was likely to have often to endure Conservative governments that had only minority support north of the border, as happened in 1970–74 and would be the case between 1979 and 1997. Having devolved self-government with significant economic powers was thus a way of insulating Scotland from the negative effects of UK Conservative governments and also a way of pursuing in Scotland more radical policies than the rest of the UK regardless of the political complexion of the government of the day in London. As early as 1972, the then general secretary, James Jack, expressed his support for devolution in the following terms: 'I say to those who respond to the suggestion of a Scottish Parliament, I am all for it because . . . there is not the slightest doubt in my mind that a Scottish Parliament would be a workers' Parliament'.[38]

Despite the fact that the STUC as a whole was strongly supportive of self-government, a minority, concentrated in some unions, remained opposed to devolution. Their argument was two-fold. First, government policy was based on a fundamental misunderstanding of what Scotland really wanted, hence economic problems had to be tackled through a change of policy at the UK level rather than by devolving some non-crucial powers to a Scottish assembly.[39] Secondly, the strategy of pursuing devolution in order to counter the attraction of independence was a foolish one, for it was likely to lead to the opposite outcome. As a delegate to the 1976 Congress said: 'we are trying to appease a movement with an insatiable appetite, which can only be satisfied with the complete separation from England and the break-up of the United Kingdom'.[40]

The STUC's opposition to independence, on the other hand, appears to have been primarily determined by economic factors though hostility to the nationalist ideology also played a part. The STUC was very critical of the SNP's argument that oil reserves in the NorthSea had made Scottish independence economically advantageous, on the basis that oil was not enough to solve Scotland's economic problems and that secession would have been extremely costly for the Scottish working class. Independence was thus rejected because its economic costs were perceived as far outweighing any benefits that may have derived from it. At the 1976 Congress the STUC carried a motion declaring: 'we are convinced that Scotland's economic and social problems will only be solved within the U.K. framework'[41] and that 'we have consistently argued that separatism would be detrimental to the people of Scotland and could only lead to a deterioration in the quality of life of the Scottish people'.[42] The following year, the position was reiterated using these words: 'to go it alone would lead to untold disaster. Scotland's inter-dependence on the rest of the U.K. ranges right across the economic spectrum'.[43] Moreover, the STUC was hostile to nationalism itself, which it portrayed as 'the old cockerel crowing on his own dunghill, representing the politics of greed, selfishness and self-interest, the very betrayal of Scotland's greatest heritage'.[44] In consequence, it was also deeply hostile to the SNP and, in particular, to the latter's strategy of supporting devolution as a stepping-stone to secession. At the 1976 Congress, the STUC denounced the SNP as 'those vocal, strident and divisive people whose only interest in an Assembly is to use it as a short-cut to a separate state'[45] and one of the delegates said that 'I imagine very few delegates at this Congress would want to walk the same corridors as that particular political party'.[46]

The STUC strategy on self-government was thus based on the exploitation of its privileged position as both a national and a class organisation to claim a mandate to 'speak for Scotland', as 'the most representative organ of Scottish opinion',[47] to pursue institutional and ideological advantage. The self-government issue offered the STUC the opportunity to do so and to advance policy objectives which would benefit the sectors of the population represented by the Congress, on the assumption that the policy output of a Scottish government would be closer to the STUC's preferences than the output of the British government. In particular, devolved Scottish government with responsibilities over significant portions of economic policy would have helped insulate Scotland from the negative effects of the economic policy of a British Conservative government.

Perception and strategic use of the EU

The STUC, like the wider British trades union movement, had a deeply negative perception of the European Union in the 1970s. Before and during the negotiations on membership it was opposed to the UK joining the European Union.[48] Afterwards, it adopted a policy of boycotting the EU institutions – specifically the Economic and Social Committee where the representatives of trades unions sat – and strongly supported the Labour party's policy of re-negotiation of the terms of membership. At the time of the 1975 referendum the question of EU membership was of the utmost importance for the STUC and the organisation vigorously campaigned for a No vote.[49] The STUC's position was clearly expressed by the motion carried at the 1975 Congress whose mover declared: 'there was no issue more important in this Congress than to make the strongest call to the people of Scotland to vote "No" on June 5th, and to mean it, to organise every day in every way and every working place, in every street, until independence day arrived'.[50]

After the victory of the Yes side in the referendum, the STUC shifted the focus of its activities from mobilising support for UK withdrawal towards maximising the representation of trades unions' interests in policy-making at the Union level. Its principal objective was to secure direct representation for the STUC in the Economic and Social Committee. However, this was not possible at the time as all the seats allocated to the UK had been filled by the British TUC. Faute de mieux, a permanent consultation mechanism between the Scottish and the British TUCs was agreed.[51] However, the STUC quickly grew disappointed by its ability – and that of the European trades unions in general – to significantly influence the EU decision-making process and extract advantages for the working classes. As a result, in the late 1970s it resumed its previous policy of advocating British withdrawal. At the 1976 Congress a motion carried unanimously stated that 'this Congress reaffirms its fundamental opposition to the objectives of the E.E.C'.[52] Two years later a motion remitted to the General Council declared: 'this Congress agrees that our continued membership of the European Economic Community has been a political and economic disaster for the British people'.[53] Thus, the STUC's general attitude at the time of the 1979 referendum can be neatly summarised by what a mover of a motion carried by a substantial majority at that year's congress said: 'when talking about the Common Market one of the great difficulties I find is curtailing what you want to say against it because so much of it is bad'.[54]

The STUC's negative perception of the European Union in the 1970s was determined by two groups of factors. On the one hand, the STUC was opposed to the nature of the EU in economic and political terms. On the other hand, there were concerns on the effect of the EU's policies on Scotland. Within each group, a number of factors were at play. Starting with the attitude to the EU in general terms, it is possible to identify three main elements. The first was opposition to the nature of European economic integration as defined by the objectives of the Treaty of Rome, in particular freedom of movement for capital. Given these objectives, the STUC saw the European Union as a capitalist organisation that was strengthening the power of owners of capital, especially large multi-national companies, vis-à-vis the working classes and government as it gave the former the ability to shift production anywhere in the EU while taking advantage of the common market.[55] As the principle was one of the cornerstones of the Treaty of Rome, the STUC was also acutely aware that no degree of renegotiation could have changed the capitalist nature of the EU, hence its support for UK withdrawal.

Closely related to the previous motive was the perception that the EU was an instrument of the Western alliance aimed at stifling socialism domestically and at antagonising the socialist countries of Eastern Europe internationally.[56] This aspect too could not be changed by re-negotiation of the terms of membership as the Treaty of Rome would remain the essence of the EU: 'No matter how one looked at it, the Treaty of Rome was against socialism and the Treaty could only be amended if every other member in the Market agreed, which meant virtually that it was impossible to change the Rome Treaty'.[57]

Thirdly, the STUC perceived the EU as an organisation both non-democratic and anti-democratic. Non-democratic because it was ruled by unelected bureaucrats not facing any real democratic accountability and anti-democratic because the principle that EU law over-rides state law undermined the democratic process in the UK. As a motion carried at the 1975 Congress put it, EU membership was a subversion of democracy and 'a rolling back of British history'.[58] In particular, this was so because, by under-mining the democratic process at state level, it crucially weakened the trades unions' influence on public policy: 'to support Common Market member-ship was inconsistent with the Unions' stand to be consulted and to partic-ipate in decisions by Governments which affect our economy'.[59] The prospect of direct elections to the European Parliament, far from being a step towards the democratisation of the EU, was seen as a further threat to British democracy.[60]

The second group of determinants of the STUC's hostility was related to the perception of the impact of EU policies on Scotland. Criticism was directed at three policies in particular: market integration, agricultural policy and fisheries policy; but also included, remarkably, the developing European Regional Development Fund (ERDF). As regards market integration, the STUC repeatedly denounced the fact that the ability to move capital freely within the EU had generated drainage of capital from the UK to the conti-nent. In other words, capital moved only one way, away from the UK and into the other EU countries.[61] Scotland had most to lose from such drainage as it already faced dramatic difficulties in preventing capital from leaving Scotland for more attractive opportunities in central and southern England.

The STUC was also highly critical of the effects that the financing of the Common Agricultural Policy (CAP) and of the EU budget had on Scotland. The CAP was perceived as a shamefully wasteful policy, deliberately favouring continental farmers and contrary to the interest of Scottish farmers and working people.[62] Scottish farmers were benefiting less than their continental or even English counterparts from the CAP as the latter was targeted towards produce which were marginal in Scotland. Moreover, as the mechanisms of the CAP were imposing artificially high food prices, the policy was exacting a heavy price on the Scottish working class, for whom food was a major item of expen-diture. Similar criticism was directed at the effects of the Common Fisheries Policy (CFP) on the fishing industry in Scotland. By allowing other EU fleets to fish in Scottish waters, the CFP was accused of having devastated the Scottish fishing industry.[63] Remarkably, the STUC was also opposed to the efforts to transform the original ERDF into a 'European regional policy' on the grounds that the UK's regional problems were radically different from those prevailing on the continent and because the inter-governmental method 'gives Government the maximum freedom, and the Commission the minimum basis for interference'.[64]

Given this deep hostility towards the European Union, it is not surprising that the STUC, far from perceiving the EU as offering opportunities and incentives for self-government, perceived it as incompatible with this in principle and as posing constraints in practice. The incompatibility stemmed from inherent conflict between the perceived nature of the EU and the reasons for demanding self-government seen above. The STUC's demand for a Scottish assembly was primarily determined by the desire to democratise the Scottish political system and to give it the ability to pursue autonomous economic policies. The achievement of both objectives was deemed threatened by membership of the EU as the latter was eroding the democratic process at state level and was putting ever-larger constraints on the conduct of economic policy. In short, within the EU, 'any argument about a Scottish Assembly with powers would be purely academic'.[65] A stronger version of this argument was that a Scottish Assembly was necessary in order to implement in Scotland policies which were more left-wing than those offered from London, while the EU was imposing on both the UK as a whole, and Scotland in particular, policies which were more right-wing than the British ones. As a delegate at the 1976 Congress put it, 'How can the S.T.U.C. argue for meaningful Scottish Devolution and accept a situation where a group of monopoly capitalists in Brussels can overrule the will of the people of this country?'[66]

The fact that two major areas of competence that the STUC wanted conferred on a Scottish assembly – agriculture and fisheries – were also those in which EU competence was wider and deeper was also perceived as placing practical constraints on, rather than offering opportunities for, self-govern-ment, though the STUC believed that those constraints would not be insur-mountable.[67] Not even the nascent regional policy was perceived as offering opportunities. The STUC was aware of its potential importance for Scotland and of the need to adequately represent Scottish interests in that arena, but the issue was not used as an additional element in the case for self-govern-ment; rather as a natural consequence of the establishment of an assembly. One year after the setting up of the ERDF, in early 1976, the STUC's General Council agreed 'on the need to examine means to ensuring that S.T.U.C. views on matters of such crucial importance to Scotland are heard in Brussels'.[68] The same approach was taken on the wider issue of repre-senting general Scottish interests at the EU level: a motion remitted to the General Council at the 1977 Congress demanded 'an assurance that in any consultations in Europe and the E.E.C. on matters devolved to the Scottish assembly, there will be separate representation of Scottish interests'[69] but did not use the question of the representation of Scottish interests as an addi-tional reason for demanding self-government. This contrasts sharply with the way this issue was used by the Church of Scotland, as seen above. In sum, the STUC perceived the EU as, at the same time, exacerbating the negative aspects of the UK system and undermining the positive ones. As Aitken put it, it 'saw Brussels at the time as an even less palatable source of subjugation than Westminster'.[70] The STUC was thus deeply hostile towards the EU, it perceived it as antithetical to meaningful regional self-government and it did not utilise the European dimension in its strategy to achieve devolution.

The business organisations

The representation of business interests in Scotland was carried out by a number of umbrella groups, some of which were semi-autonomous units of the corresponding UK-wide groups. The latter case was that of the Confederation of British Industry (Scotland) and the Institute of Directors (Scotland) while the Scottish Chambers of Commerce and the Federation of Small Businesses were autonomous Scottish bodies. Most of these groups had close links with the Conservative party. For the purposes of the present analysis the various groups are treated as a unitary actor.

Self-government policy

Scottish business was very strongly opposed to devolution and even more strongly opposed to independence in the period under examination. As early as 1976, the main business organisations joined a campaigning group called *Keep Britain United*, originally established within the Conservative party, which later changed its name to *Scotland Is British* and which remained close to the Conservative party, though not formally part of it. Throughout the period, business organisations opposed the devolution policy of the Labour government and played a prominent role in the *Scotland Says No* group during the 1979 referendum campaign. Indeed, the amount of financial resources mobilised by individual companies and umbrella groups for the No campaign was a key determinant of the fact that the latter was significantly better funded than the Yes campaign. Some authors consider this a crucial factor that determined the greater effectiveness of the No campaign and thus, ultimately, the referendum result.[71] The organisations grouped within *Scotland Is British* defended their decision to take part in the debate on self-government against accusations of interference in political matters on the following ground: 'to this we answer that if the future unity of our country is at stake, then the issue is far more than a political one – it is a major constitutional issue like joining Europe, which is as much a business concern as anyone else's'.[72] They explicitly stated that they intended to mobilise public opinion about what was at stake in devolution, in the belief that 'the more people are becoming aware of what is involved, the less they like it'.[73]

Two main factors determined business hostility towards self-government. Firstly, devolution was seen as likely to generate extra costs, possibly higher taxes and an additional layer of government without bringing any tangible benefit to the Scottish economy and its actors. Although not explicitly stated, the underlying factor was the traditionally negative attitude towards government intervention in the economy among Scottish business.[74] Secondly, but crucially, business strongly opposed devolution because it believed that the demand for devolution had been fuelled by nationalistic ideology and that, therefore, devolution was bound to lead to secession. In an article setting out the position of business organisations on devolution, the president of the Glasgow Chamber of Commerce and prominent leader of the *Scotland Is British* group despised what he called 'narrow and emotional nationalism' and made clear that business opposed devolution because they felt it would inevitably lead to independence and saw the SNP's support for devolution as confirming their suspicions: 'We believe and fear that the creation of a directly elected assembly will lead almost inevitably to separation . . . these are views which the separatists share and they are, moreover, their objectives. We agree with them that independence is the only outcome'.[75] The same view was expressed by Douglas Hardie, a former chairman of the Scottish CBI. In an article published in the last stages of the campaign, he pointed out that the SNP was the only party united in support for devolution and argued: 'they [the SNP] are campaigning strongly in favour of a "yes" vote, because they believe that it would be easier to achieve this goal with the Scotland Act 1978 than without it. I believe that they are right'.[76] A survey of the largest Scottish companies carried out by the *Glasgow Herald* during the campaign also showed that although the business sector was critical of devolution in general and of the Scotland Act 1978 in particular, the fundamental determinant of its hostility was the fear that devolution would lead to the break-up of the UK and that this would have had disastrous consequences, not least because it would have involved withdrawal from the European Union.[77] As the president of the Glasgow Chamber of Commerce put it: 'in the event of separation, our home market is cut by 70%, and trading with Europe would be disastrously affected'.[78]

Perception and strategic use of the EU

Scottish business was strongly supportive of EU membership in the 1970s. The UK-wide rationale, i.e. that membership would improve the competitive position of British industry and facilitate trade with the continent, was reinforced in the case of Scotland by the fact that the Scottish economy was proportionally more dependent on exports than the English one and that continental Europe was a particularly important market for industries such as whisky. As a rule, Scottish business also perceived European integration in positive terms as an internationalist, outward-looking process.

On the basis of this positive attitude towards the EU and the hostility towards self-government analysed above, the business organisations perceived the demand for Scottish self-government as running counter to the process of European integration and used the European dimension to undermine the case for the former. They did so in three main ways. In general terms, business organisations feared that, given the hostility towards the EU on the part of Labour and the SNP, devolution would lead to Scotland seceding from the UK and withdrawing from the European Union. That scenario, as seen above, was perceived as disastrous for the Scottish economy. The attitudes towards the EU on the part of the actors demanding self-government was thus an additional reason for business to oppose devolution. The second reason was linked to traditional business suspicion of government and of the growth of government. Membership of the EU and the imminent prospect of direct elections to the European Parliament had already increased the levels of government business had to deal with and a Scottish assembly was perceived as increasing these even further by adding another layer. A layer that, as seen above, business considered largely redundant. As Risk put it, 'if European elections take place, with an assembly there will be five layers of elected authorities affecting the government of Scotland'.[79] Lastly, but most importantly, the business organisations exploited the European dimension to undermine the legitimacy of the demand for self-government on the grounds that Scottish nationalism was at odds with the historical trend of transcending national barriers and integrating markets at the heart of European integration. As Risk argued: 'we did not object to Brussels, nor should we to Luxembourg [Luxembourg was then perceived to be the home of the elected European Parliament] but these are in the causes of supra- and not introverted and parochial nationalism'.[80] The European dimension was thus perceived as placing constraints on Scottish self-government, at least on a normative level, and used, to a limited extent, in that guise in the business discourse against devolution.

Conclusions

The European dimension did not figure prominently in the strategies that interest groups pursued for or against self-government in the 1970s. The only actor that perceived the European dimension as offering incentives and opportunities for self-government – the Church of Scotland – was divided and virtually cut itself off from the debate in the crucial phase of the campaign. In contrast, both the STUC and the business organisations, albeit for opposite reasons, perceived the European Union as incompatible with self-government for Scotland.

It was not by coincidence that the Church of Scotland was the only actor seeing a positive connection between European integration and Scottish self-government since it was also the only one with positive attitudes towards *both* issues. As seen above, the STUC supported self-government but was hostile towards the EU while the reverse was true for business. This indicates that the perception of the connection between the EU and self-government was to a large extent a function of attitudes towards each of them being consistent. The variance in attitudes towards the EU between, in particular, the Church of Scotland and the STUC shows that its fundamental determinant was ideological rather than being based on concerns about Scotland's peripherality or criticism of specific EU policies. The evidence relative to the business organisations as well as that discussed in the previous chapter in relation to the parties supports this interpretation. Those actors sharing, to a varying extent, a socialist ideology – Labour, the STUC and the SNP – were hostile to the EU while non-socialist actors – the Liberal and Conservative parties, the Church of Scotland and business – were positive towards it.

As it was the case among parties, the linkage between devolution and independence figured prominently in the position and the discourse of the interest groups. The business organisations, which played a crucial role in the No campaign, centred their discourse on the threat that devolution would represent to Scotland's membership of the UK and on the disastrous economic consequences of independence. As discussed in the next chapter, their discourse had a profound impact on public opinion.

Notes

1 See Proctor (1983: 523) and Shanks (1996: 26).
2 See, for example, Shanks (1996: 25) and Church of Scotland (1975: 45).
3 See Shanks (1996: 20–3).
4 Church of Scotland (1975: 44).
5 Church of Scotland (1975: 44–6), see also Shanks (1996: 22).
6 See Church of Scotland (1975: 41, 1976: 10 and 1980: 105).
7 See, for instance, Church of Scotland (1975: 44; 1980: 104).
8 Wolfe, interview with the author.
9 Church of Scotland (1977: 116).
10 See Church of Scotland (1975: 44–6, 1976: 7–11, 1977: 114–17), see also Proctor (1983: 529).
11 See 'Kirk's Pulpit Ban on Devolution Message', *The Scotsman*, 23 February

1979, 'Politics and the Pulpit', *The Scotsman*, 27 February 1979 and 'Dr Herron "misrepresented" Kirk Policy', *The Scotsman*, 1 March 1979; also Proctor (1983: 536–42) and Shanks (1996: 23–5).

12 Andrew Herron, 'Another Tier that Must not Be Shed on Scotland', *Glasgow Herald*, 17 February 1979.

13 Andrew Herron was vice-president of the *Scotland Says No* campaign, see Herron (1989: 27).

14 Church of Scotland (1975: 40–3).

15 Church of Scotland (1979: 47–9).

16 Church of Scotland (1979: 49).

17 Church of Scotland (1982: 124).

18 Ibidem:122; see also (1979: 49).

19 Ibidem 122

20 Church of Scotland (1976: 10).

21 IBidem: 9.

22 Church of Scotland (1975: 41, 1977: 114, 1979: 49).

23 In the late 1970s, the STUC membership peaked at 50 per cent of the Scottish workforce. For a general introduction to the STUC, see Aitken (1997).

24 On the communist influence in the STUC, see Kellas (1989: 187) and Graham and McGrath (1991: 62).

25 See Aitken (1997: 240–1).

26 See Aitken (1997: 242) and Kellas (1989: 187).

27 On labour legislation, see Keating and Bleiman (1979: 185–6); on the retention of the plurality system, see STUC (1976: 211).

28 See STUC (1976: 202 and 1978: 247).

29 STUC (1978: 255 and 617–23).

30 See STUC (1979:172–3) and Macartney (1981).

31 See Aitken (1997: 257).

32 See 'Let Us Make Our Own Decisions!', *The Daily Record*, 20 February 1979.

33 Quoted in Sillars (1986: 36).

34 STUC (1976: 199).

35 Ibidem: 468; see also STUC (1978: 258).

36 'Let Us Make Our Own Decisions!', *The Daily Record*, 20 February 1979.

37 See STUC (1976: 210).

38 Quoted in Sillars (1986: 35)

39 STUC (1976: 473).

40 Ibidem: 475; also STUC (1977: 800).

41 STUC (1976: 471).

42 STUC (1976: 205).

43 STUC (1977: 339).

44 STUC (1976: 472).

45 Ibidem: 472; see also STUC (1978: 252).

46 STUC (1976: 474).

47 Quoted in Kellas (1989: 186) from the STUC's *Submission to Royal Commission on Trade Unions and Employers' Associations*, Glasgow, 6 May 1966.

48 See Aitken (1997: 245–6) and STUC (1974: 321).

49 See STUC (1975: 274, 471, 1976: 189).

50 STUC (1975: 471).

51 STUC (1976: 189).
52 Ibidem: 464.
53 STUC (1978: 587).
54 STUC (1979: 394).
55 See in particular STUC (1975: 472; also 481 and 484).
56 See STUC (1975: 477).
57 Ibidem: 472, 475, also STUC (1979: 396).
58 STUC (1975: 484); see also STUC (1974: 319–20, 1975: 471, 1976: 464).
59 Ibidem, all references as previous note.
60 STUC (1976: 466).
61 Ibidem: 465.
62 STUC (1974: 319).
63 STUC (1979: 395).
64 STUC (1977: 327; also 1978: 132–6).
65 STUC (1975: 476).
66 STUC (1976: 466).
67 Ibidem: 208.
68 Ibidem: 190.
69 STUC (1977: 861).
70 Aitken (1997: 246).
71 See Perman (1979: especially 57) and Balsom and McAllister (1979: especially 398).
72 Risk (1978: 125).
73 Risk (1978: 127).
74 Ibidem: 123; see also Douglas Hardie, 'Why Scots Should Reject this "Bad Package" ', *The Courier and Advertiser*, 27 February 1979 and 'Irrelevant to Needs of Industry', *The Scotsman*, 17 February 1979.
75 Risk (1978: 122).
76 See Hardie, 'Why Scots Should Reject this "Bad Package" '.
77 'Scotland's business chiefs have their say on assembly', *Glasgow Herald*, 23 February 1979.
78 Risk (1978: 123).
79 Ibidem.
80 Ibidem.

4
Public opinion

The pattern of perceptions and positions seen in the preceding chapters in relation to elite actors was largely replicated at mass public level. Voters had a clear idea of where parties stood on the self-government question and party identification was a very strong predictor of constitutional preferences and of the referendum vote. Labour and Nationalist identifiers were hostile to the EU while Liberal and Conservative identifiers were supportive. This close matching between elite discourse and public opinion substantiates the claim that the elites had the ability to profoundly shape mass attitudes, in line with the theoretical assumptions outlined in chapter 1. One of the key elements emerging from the analysis of public opinion data is that support for self-government was still above 60 per cent at the time of the referendum, despite the fact that the latter's result – taking into account the effects of the 40 per cent clause – was negative. Therefore, a large gap between support for devolution and the Yes vote existed in 1979. This can be explained by the workings of a complex causal mechanism that I term the 'interaction effect' generated by the fact that devolution was widely perceived as likely to lead to independence and voters, even most of those supporting devolution in principle, preferred the status quo to secession. The following pages present and discuss the evidence supporting this interpretation.

The demand for self-government

In this section, I present and discuss three variables and the relationship between them: importance of self-government as a political issue when voting in the general elections, support for self-government and the referendum vote. Party identification is used as the main control variable.

Self-government was perceived to be not very important in 1979. It was 'fairly important' for a third of voters, but those who thought it 'not important' outnumbered those who thought it 'extremely important' by about two

Table 4.1 Importance of self-government by party identification (column %), 1979

Q. When you were deciding about voting, how important was the general issue of the form of government for Scotland?

	Conservative	Labour	Liberal	Nationalist	All
Not important	44	37	30	9	36
Fairly important	29	36	39	23	32
Extremely important	14	15	22	56	20
Don't know	13	12	9	12	12
N	222	274	67	75	729

Source: Scottish General Election Study 1979.

to one. The issue was clearly very important for Nationalist identifiers but distinctly less so for identifiers with the UK-wide parties, with only minor differences across party identification. In terms of relative importance, self-government was behind inflation and unemployment, more or less on the same level as wage-settling but more important than North Sea oil (table 4.1).[1]

If not very intense, support for self-government was considerably broad in 1979. Aggregate support was at 61 per cent, with an overall majority in favour of devolution and 7 per cent support for independence. Given the SNP's policy towards membership of the EU, at that time independence meant secession from the UK *and* the EU. The option closest to the one embodied in the Scotland Act 1978 – an assembly – was the modal preference with 28 per cent support. The distribution of preference by party identification shows three patterns. The main pattern was the 'devolutionist' one of Labour and Liberal identifiers. Among them there was a clear two-thirds preference for devolution – with no difference between the 'assembly' and the 'Parliament' options – and minimal support for independence. Conservative identifiers appeared split between devolution and the status quo with a slight preference for the former – the assembly option in particular – and, again, minimal support for independence. The preference distribution was sharply different for Nationalists. The preferred option was devolution, though this meant overwhelmingly the 'Parliament' option, while independence, somewhat surprisingly, only attracted 37 per cent support (table 4.2).

In contrast to the strength of support for self-government, the referendum result was much less positive. The Yes and No votes were at the same level of about a third of electorate each but those who did not vote but had a preference were twice as likely to favour the No side than the Yes side.

Table 4.2 Support for self-government by party identification (column %), 1979

Q. Here are a number of suggestions* which have been made about different ways of governing Scotland. Can you tell me which one comes closest to your own view?

	Conservative	Labour	Liberal	Nationalist	All
Status quo	40	20	25	5	26
Devolution	46	62	66	45	54
Assembly	29	31	33	9	28
Parliament	17	31	33	36	26
Independence	3	4	2	37	7
Self-					
government	49	66	67	82	61
Don't know	11	14	8	13	13
N	222	274	67	75	729

Note: *No devolution or Scottish assembly of any sort; Have Scottish Committees of the House of Commons come up to Scotland for their meetings; An elected Scottish assembly which would handle some Scottish affairs and would be responsible to Parliament at Westminster; A Scottish Parliament which would handle most Scottish affairs, including many economic affairs, leaving the Westminster Parliament responsible only for defence, foreign policy and international economic policy; A completely independent Scotland with a Scottish Parliament. I collapsed the first two original categories into the 'status quo' category.
Source: Scottish Election Study 1979.

Bearing in mind the existence of the 40 per cent clause and the way it had been exploited, it is likely that many opponents of devolution stayed at home in the belief that it would have been equivalent to voting No. These data indicate that the result of the 1979 referendum was a clear, albeit narrow, rejection of devolution even though the actual referendum result showed a slight positive margin. The voting pattern by party identification showed a continuum from the Conservatives at one extreme and the Nationalists at the other with Liberal and Labour identifiers in between, respectively. Including those who did not vote but had a preference, 68 per cent of Conservative identifiers and 51 per cent of Liberal ones opposed the Act. On the opposite side of the spectrum, 46 per cent of Labour and fully 80 per cent of Nationalist identifiers endorsed it. Further evidence for this conclusion is provided by voters' own interpretation of the referendum result with a clear plurality interpreting it as indicating that Scots did not really want an assembly (tables 4.3 and 4.4).

There was thus a wide gap between public support and the referendum vote created, by definition, by a large number of supporters of self-government voting No in the referendum. Taking into account those who did not vote but

Table 4.3 Referendum vote by party identification (column %), 1979

Q. Did you vote in the recent referendum on Devolution for Scotland? If yes did you vote 'Yes' or 'No'? If no did you favour the 'Yes' side or the 'No' side?

	Conservative	Labour	Liberal	Nationalist	All
Voted No	56	24	36	3	33
Didn't vote					
favoured No	12	12	15	4	11
(Total No)	(68)	(36)	(51)	(7)	(44)
Didn't vote					
no pref.	4	8	5	4	6
Voted Yes	15	39	31	69	33
Didn't vote					
favoured Yes	13	7	6	11	6
(Total Yes)	(28)	(46)	(37)	(80)	(39)
Don't know/					
no answer	10	11	7	9	11
N	222	274	67	75	729

Source: Scottish Election Study 1979.

Table 4.4 Interpretation of the referendum result by party identification (column %), 1979

Q. In your own opinion, did the referendum result show that the Scottish people wanted an Assembly or not?

Weight/Category	Conservative	Labour	Liberal	Nationalist	All
−1 Did not want					
assembly	60	38	42	15	42
0 Indecisive result	14	14	15	19	15
1 Wanted					
assembly	15	36	33	56	30
Don't know/					
no answer	12	13	10	11	13
N	222	274	67	75	729
Index*	**−45**	**−2**	**−9**	**41**	**−12**

Note: *index varies between −100 = 100% of respondents thought Scots did not want an assembly and +100 = 100% of respondents thought they wanted an assembly.
Source: Scottish Election Study 1979.

had a preference, more than one in three supporters of self-government opposed the Scotland Act 1978. If the data are broken down by the preferred option supported, however, we can observe sharply different voting patterns. Virtual supporters of independence voted overwhelmingly Yes or favoured the Yes side, as did two-thirds of those virtually in favour of the Parliament option. In stark contrast, a majority of virtual supporters of the assembly option actually voted No – or favoured a No vote – in the referendum. Therefore, we are confronted with the paradox that those theoretically in favour of the option closest to the one put to the vote in the referendum were, remarkably, those most responsible for voting against it (table 4.5). Controlling for party identification shows that if the gap was widest among Conservative identifiers, a substantial 41 per cent of Labour identifiers who supported the assembly option also voted No or favoured a No vote.[2]

Is there evidence that an 'interaction effect' between attitudes to devolution and attitudes to independence was at play? Starting with the connection between devolution and independence, the data indicate that devolution was indeed perceived as highly likely to lead to independence. A break-up of the UK was cited as the most important disadvantage of devolution, even if devolution by itself, of course, would not have broken up the UK. Moreover, those in favour of the status quo or the 'assembly' option were much more likely to fear it than those supporting the 'Parliament' option and independence (table 4.6).

Table 4.5 Referendum vote of supporters of self-government (column %), 1979

1979: Did you vote in the recent referendum on Devolution for Scotland? If Yes did you vote 'Yes' or 'No' If No did you favour the 'Yes' side or the 'No' side?

| | Devolution | | Independence | All |
	Assembly	*Parliament*		
Voted Yes	36	57	68	49
Didn't vote				
favoured Yes	6	10	12	8
(Total Yes)	(42)	(67)	(80)	(57)
Didn't vote				
no preference	5	8	8	7
Didn't vote				
favoured No	14	9	2	10
Voted No	39	16	10	26
(Total No)	(53)	(25)	(12)	(36)
N	205	189	50	444

Source: Scottish Election Study 1979.

Attitudes to independence itself were deeply negative across party identifications, with the only partial exception of Nationalist identifiers. Around 70 per cent of both Conservative and Liberal identifiers were 'very much against' it and only 49 per cent of Nationalists were very much in favour (table 4.7).

Moreover, attitudes to independence were more negative than to the status quo. Significantly, a very minor change to the latter such as having Scottish MPs meeting in Scotland was strongly preferred to independence and even no change at all in the way Scotland was governed was still preferred to independence. Once again, the pattern was reinforced among virtual supporters of the 'assembly' option. Not only did the latter largely prefer no change at all to independence but they even had a slightly positive

Table 4.6 Most important disadvantage of devolution by constitutional preference (column %), 1979

Q. Which one of these is the most important disadvantage of devolution?

Disadvantage	Status quo	Assembly	Parliament	Independence	All
Break-up UK	38	37	23	16	27
Cost of bureaucracy	25	22	25	28	22
Too many levels of govt	16	18	16	16	15
Benefits wrong	5	10	11	8	8
Harm economy	9	6	4	2	5
Loss UK voice	4	6	6	10	5
Others/don't know	3	1	15	20	18

Note: N = 729.
Source: Scottish Election Study 1979.

Table 4.7 Attitudes to independence by party identification (column %), 1979

Q. For each suggestion* on the card, could you say whether you are very much in favour, somewhat in favour, somewhat against or very much against that suggestion?

Suggestion	Conservative	Labour	Liberal	Nationalist	All
Very much against	71	54	69	9	56
Somewhat against	11	17	18	13	15
Somewhat in favour	3	9	1	16	6
Very much in favour	2	7	3	49	9
Don't know/no answer	13	13	9	12	13
N	222	274	67	75	729

Note: *in this case: 'a completely independent Scotland with a Scottish Parliament'.
Source: Scottish Election Study 1979.

Table 4.8 Attitudes to the status quo and to independence among supporters of devolution (indices*), 1979

Q. For each suggestion† on the card, could you say whether you are very much in favour, somewhat in favour, somewhat against or very much against that suggestion?

Suggestion	Assembly	Parliament	All
Status quo 1**	−91	−110	−100
Status quo 2**	17	−30	−3
Independence	−163	−87	−126

Notes: N = 394; †see note at table 2; *indices vary from −200 = 100% of respondents were 'very much against' and +200 = 100% of respondents were 'very much in favour'; **there were two options which largely amounted to maintaining the status quo in the 1979 survey, see note at table 4.2.
Source: Scottish Election Study 1979.

attitude towards the option of having Scottish MPs meeting in Scotland (table 4.8).

The final piece of evidence is provided by the responses to the question of the role of the SNP in the politics of self-government. Conservative, Labour and, to a lesser extent, Liberal identifiers were up to twice as likely to think that the SNP delayed devolution by frightening off those who feared separation than to think it speeded up devolution and a substantial 32 per cent of Nationalist identifiers thought likewise (table 4.9).

Attitudes towards the UK and the EU

To measure mass attitudes towards the UK political system, I employ three variables: satisfaction with government, perception of Scotland's welfare and identification with the UK. The first variable measures whether respondents were satisfied with the performance of the UK system of government. The second variable measures whether Scotland was perceived to be economically better off or worse off than other regions of the UK. This variable is used to provide an estimation of the public satisfaction with the ability of the UK political system to deliver economic prosperity equally to all areas of the state. Finally, identification with the UK measures to what extent Scots identified themselves primarily with the UK as opposed to identifying themselves primarily with Scotland, in other words whether their primary national identity was British or Scottish. These three measures are intended to capture the three dimensions of support for a political system: the political dimension, the economic one and the symbolic-affective one.

Table 4.9 Perceived effect of SNP on devolution by party identification (column %), 1979

Q. Whether or not you yourself ever voted for the SNP, what effect do you think the SNP has had on devolution?

Weight/Category	Conservative	Labour	Liberal	Nationalist	All
−1 Delayed devolution by frightening off those who feared separation	45	38	39	32	38
0 Not much effect	24	29	22	16	25
1 Speeded up moves towards devolution	19	19	28	40	23
0 Don't know	12	14	11	12	14
N	222	274	67	75	729
Index*	**−26**	**−19**	**−11**	**8**	**−15**

Notes: N = 729; *index varies from −100 = 100% of respondents thought the SNP had delayed devolution and +100 = 100% of respondents thought the SNP had speeded up devolution. *Source*: Scottish Election Study 1979.

The data show a great deal of variation both across measures and across party identifications. The aggregate pattern combined a fair degree of satisfaction with government with a deeply negative perception of Scotland's welfare vis-à-vis the rest of the UK and a primary identification with Scotland rather than with Britain. The perception of Scotland as being poorer than the other areas was consistently held by all party identifiers. On the two other measures, however, the Conservatives, at one end of the spectrum, were very satisfied with the way the UK political system worked and were marginally more likely to feel primarily British rather than Scottish whereas Nationalist identifiers, at the other end, had deeply negative attitudes to all three aspects. Labour and Liberal identifiers displayed a broadly similar pattern of satisfaction with government but a negative perception of Scotland's welfare and primary identification with Scotland (table 4.10).

Only one variable of attitudes towards the European Union is available for 1979: a generic measure of support. It is reasonable to assume that this variable effectively measures the respondent's perception of Scotland's membership of the EU, thus making it comparable to a variable on satisfaction with membership available for 1997. On this measure, Scottish voters had an overall negative perception of the EU in 1979 though significant variation between party identifications existed. Conservative and, narrowly, Liberal identifiers were positive while Labour and, especially, Nationalist identifiers were hostile (table 4.11).

Table 4.10 Attitudes to the UK by party identification (indices), 1979

Satisfaction with government:†
Q. How many marks out of ten would you give the following . . . the Westminster
Parliament?
Perception of Scotland's welfare:
Q. Compared with other parts of Britain, would do you say that Scotland was better
off or not so well off ?
Identification with the UK:
Q. Do you consider yourself to be British or Scottish or English or Irish or
something else? If you *had* to choose, which would you say you were?

Attitude	Conservative	Labour	Liberal	Nationalist	All
Satisfaction with govt*†	87	26	46	−45	40
Scotland's welfare**	−55	−71	−65	−78	−66
Identification with the UK***	3	−22	−12	−68	−16

Notes: †for the sake of tractability, I re-grouped the original categories into four categories on
the basis of the following conversion: 9, 10 = works extremely well; 6, 7, 8 = could be
improved in small ways; 3, 4, 5 = could be improved quite a lot; 0, 1, 2 = needs a great deal of
improvement; *index varies between −200 = all respondents were very dissatisfied and
+200 = all respondents were very satisfied; **index varies between −100 = 100% of
respondents thought Scotland was worse off than the rest of the UK and +100 = 100% of
respondents thought Scotland was better off; ***index varies between −100 = primary
identification with Scotland and +100 = primary identification with the UK.
Source: Scottish General Election Study 1979.

Determinants of the referendum vote

I tested the correlations between the referendum vote and eleven explanatory
variables in logistic regressions. This multi-variate statistical technique enables
the researcher to test the association between a number of independent variables and a dichotomous dependent variable, in this case the vote in the 1979
referendum. A statistically significant positive association between a given
category against the 'base' category for each independent variable indicates
that voters possessing that characteristic were more likely than those in the
'base' category to have voted No rather than Yes in the referendum.

In addition to party identification and the standard sociological variables
(class, identity and religion), the other variables have been selected to test
whether the following factors had an independent effect in generating a No
vote: support for self-government (constitutional preferences), fear of secession (attitudes to independence, disadvantage of devolution), Scotland's
economic deprivation (Scotland's welfare), government un/popularity
(proxied by attitudes to Callaghan, the Prime Minister), dis/satisfaction with

Table 4.11 Attitudes to the EU by party identification column[1], 1979

Q. How many marks out of ten would you give the following . . . the Common Market?

Attitude	Conservative	Labour	Liberal	Nationalist	All
Negative	15	37	25	56	31
Neither	45	34	34	20	36
Positive	29	16	28	13	21
Don't know/na	11	13	12	11	11
N	222	274	67	75	729

Note: for the sake of tractability and comparability with the 1997 data, I re-grouped the original categories into three categories on the basis of the following conversion: 7, 8, 9, 10 = good for Scotland; 4, 5, 6 = neither good nor bad; 0, 1, 2, 3 = bad for Scotland.
Source: Scottish General Election Study 1979.

the UK political system (attitudes to Westminster) and dis/satisfaction with the EU (attitudes to the EU).

The results indicate that only four variables – and three 'factors' – had a statistically significant independent effect on the No vote. As expected, the vote was profoundly shaped by partisanship. Conservative identifiers were much more likely than Labour identifiers to have voted No whereas Nationalist identifiers were much less likely to have done so. The correlation is weaker and not statistically significant, however, for Liberal identifiers. However powerful partisanship was, though, it was not the only determinant. Attitudes towards self-government also had a strong effect not entirely mediated by partisanship. Supporters of the status quo were much more likely to have voted No than those in favour of an assembly.[3] Less intuitively, but more importantly for the argument advanced in this book, fear of secession had a powerful independent effect on the No vote, comparable in strength to that of partisanship. Those 'very much against' independence were much more likely to have voted No than those just 'against' it. Secessionists on the other hand, especially 'strong' ones, were much more likely to have voted Yes, though the correlations are not statistically significant. Moreover, a fear that devolution would lead to the 'break-up of the UK' was also a powerful independent factor in producing a No vote.

In contrast, neither the perception of Scotland's economic deprivation nor dis/satisfaction with the Labour government of Prime Minister Callaghan had a meaningful impact, either substantively or statistically. Attitudes to the UK political system and to the EU did not have a clear effect – let alone an independent one – beyond the fact that those very dissatisfied with the former and, to a lesser extent, with the latter appear to have been less

Table 4.12 Logistic regression models of No voting in the 1979 referendum

	Model 1	Model 2
Party identification (base: Labour)		
Conservative	1.279***	1.388***
Liberal	0.236	0.455
Nationalist	−1.910*	−1.889*
Constitutional preferences (base: assembly)		
Status quo	2.066***	1.851***
Parliament	−0.840*	−0.822**
Independence	2.566	3.060
Attitudes to independence (base: against)		
Very much against	1.334***	1.325***
Favour	−0.218	−0.276
Very much favour	−2.632	−3.397*
Disadvantage of devolution (base: other/ don't know)		
Too many levels of government	0.654	0.657
More bureaucracy	0.813*	0.696*
Break-up of the UK	0.994**	0.947**
Scotland's welfare (base: same)		
Better off than the rest of the UK	−0.985	
Not so well off as the rest of the UK	−0.753	
Attitudes to Callaghan† (base: very good)		
Good	0.017	
Bad	−0.57	
Very bad	−0.41	
Attitudes to Westminster† (base: very good)		
Good	0.642	
Bad	0.245	
Very bad	−1.307	
Attitudes to the EU† (base: very good)		
Good	0.278	
Bad	0.373	
Very bad	−0.160	
Class (base: working)		
Middle	0.721	
None/don't know	0.599	
National identity (base: Scottish)		
British	0.132	
Religion (base: Church of Scottland)		
Roman Catholic	0.497	
Constant	−2.642	−2.039
−2 log likelihood	384.360	409.945
Pseudo-r^2 (Nagelkerke)	0.596	0.556
Percentage correctly predicted	80.6	80.2

Table 4.12 (continued)

Notes: the 'don't know' categories were included in the analysis but results are not reported here for the sake of brevity; †I re-grouped the original ten categories into four categories on the basis of the following conversion: 9, 10 = very good; 6, 7, 8 = good; 3, 4, 5 = bad; 0, 1, 2 = very bad. ***significant at $p < 0.001$; **significant at $p < 0.01$; *significant at $p < 0.05$. Interaction effects among the explanatory variables were tested for and found not significant, the results are not reported here but are available from the author.

likely to have voted No. The sociological variables including, somewhat surprisingly, national identity had no clear effect on the vote either. Lastly, the crucial role of the first four variables is also confirmed by the fact that a model restricted to them is able to correctly predict almost as many cases as the full model (table 4.12).

Conclusions

As these results show, the 1979 referendum vote was determined in a complex way. Three crucial aspects emerge. First, support for self-government was well above the majority threshold at the time of the referendum. Notwithstanding this, the 'real' result – taking into account the preferences and the behaviour of those who did not vote but had an opinion – was a clear rejection of the Scotland Act 1978. There was thus a wide gap between support and the referendum vote created by a large number of voters theoretically in favour of self-government who decided to vote No. The bulk of these voters paradoxically supported the 'assembly' option – i.e. the one on offer – while supporters of greater devolution or independence by and large voted Yes. The negative outcome of the referendum was thus produced by a large number of devolutionists who turned against the Scotland Act 1978.

Why did they do so? Partisanship explains this only partially: many Labour and Liberal devolutionists also voted No. The data show that fear of secession was a key factor. Voters perceived a very close link between devolution and independence: they saw the former as highly likely to lead to the latter. Moreover, crucially, devolutionists viewed secession in a very negative light and preferred the status quo to it. As they thought that devolution would facilitate secession, a significant number of them are likely to have come to view the referendum vote as a choice between the status quo and secession. Faced with this ultimate choice, they chose the status quo.

Lastly, most of the other explanatory variables discussed in the literature do not appear to have played a significant role in shaping the vote. This is true, in particular, of the alleged unpopularity of the Callaghan government[4] and also of the widespread feeling of Scotland's relative economic deprivation vis-à-vis the rest of the UK. Likewise, attitudes to the UK political system and to the EU were largely mediated by partisanship so did not have a significant direct impact on the vote. Though support for the UK political system among pro-self-government voters was higher than support for the EU, the two variables were broadly associated and negatively correlated with support for self-government. This suggests that voters supporting self-government perceived the EU as a 'negative extension' of the UK in 1979.

Notes

1 See Dardanelli (2002: 334).
2 See Dardanelli (2002: 336).
3 The unexpected – positive – sign of the correlation with support for independence is likely to have been produced by the very small number of cases.
4 In contrast to England, Labour's popularity increased in Scotland between 1974 and 1979, see Dardanelli (2002: 260).

5
Failed Europeanisation in the 1970s

As seen in this first part of the book, the European dimension had a minimal impact on the politics of self-government in the 1970s. Most elite actors – notably those pro-devolution – saw few connections between the two issues and did not utilise the European dimension in their campaigns. By so doing they failed to allay fears among the mass public about the link between devolution and independence and the very negative view of the latter. The failure to Europeanise the politics of self-government meant that the latter remained a two-level, as opposed to a three-level, game in which the Yes side was at a structural disadvantage vis-à-vis its opponents. It thus loomed large in the defeat of devolution in the referendum.

Elite actors

As discussed below, there are three main aspects in the elite actors' failure to Europeanise self-government in the 1970s.[1] First, they perceived the European Union in a negative way, as a centralising, undemocratic and capitalist organisation which was deeply threatening for Scotland. Second, largely due to this hostility, they saw little connection between the European dimension and their demand for self-government. The only connections that were identified were of a negative association, i.e. European integration running counter to Scotland's aspirations to self-government. As a consequence, third, they did not utilise the European dimension to build a positive and 'progressive' image of devolution and of independence at mass public level and remained vulnerable to the attacks of the No side.

Negative perception of the EU

The first and most fundamental factor was that the key actors pursuing self-government – the SNP, the Labour party and the STUC – had a negative perception of the European Union. They perceived the EU as a 'negative extension' of the UK, i.e. reinforcing the negative aspects of the latter. This perception was crystallised on two aspects in particular. The type of economic integration pursued by the European Union based on free trade and market liberalisation was perceived as damaging the working classes and the peripheral areas to the advantage of the capital-owners and of the core areas. The supra-national character of the EU system and the indirect legitimation of its policy-making were perceived to lead to further centralisation of power and erosion of democratic accountability. The evidence suggests that the former aspect was the dominant one. The only exceptions to this pattern on the pro-self-government side were the Liberal party, the Church of Scotland and, to a lesser extent, media actors such as *The Scotsman* and the *Glasgow Herald*.[2] These actors did not show a perception of the EU as a 'negative extension' of the UK and, especially in the case of the Church and the Liberals, were broadly positive towards it. The stronger relative political power of the SNP, Labour and the STUC vis-à-vis the Church of Scotland, the Liberal party and the two newspapers determined that the negative perception of the EU was the domi-nant one in the pro-selfgovernment camp. The cross-actor variation in the per-ception of the European Union indicates that ideological factors were the likely determinants. As regards the perception of economic integration, this seems to have been shaped by the conception of the role of government intervention in the economy embodied in the socialist ideology shared, to a varying extent, by the Labour party, the STUC and the SNP and rejected by the Church of Scotland, *The Scotsman* and the *Glasgow Herald*. This conception was opposed to free trade and market liberalisation for the reasons mentioned above. As regards the perception of political aspects this seems to have been shaped in the case of the SNP by a nationalist ideology based on a monolithic and absolute conception of national sovereignty which was clearly at odds with the exercise of government at the supra-state level. In the case of Labour and the STUC it seems to have also been dictated by the fact that the EU level of policy-making was out of reach of the labour movement and was therefore marginalising it. In sum, due to ideological factors, the key pro-self-government actors had a neg-ative perception of the EU which was mentally located to the right of the UK system, itself being perceived to be to the right of Scotland.

EU perceived as irrelevant for self-government

As a result, the pro-self-government elite actors did not perceive the European Union as having a positive connection with their demand for Scottish self-government. In other words, they did not perceive it as a facili-tator of self-government, providing incentives/opportunities which could be used to strengthen support for self-government at mass public level. On the contrary, there was a widespread assumption that the European dimension was largely irrelevant for self-government and, insofar as a connection was identified, this tended to be negative, i.e. seeing the process of European integration as being antithetical to the quest for Scottish self-government. The opposite perception, of regional self-government being a logical consequence of, or even a counter-balance to, supra-state integration was confined to academic circles and to the most 'intellectual' and analytically minded political actors. Importantly, the prevailing perception of a negative association between integration and self-government was shared by the pro- and anti- self-government camps. The former saw Scottish self-government as antithetical to integration because integration was perceived as a process of further political centralisation and economic liberalisation which was most damaging for peripheral regions such as Scotland.[3] The latter also saw them as being in contradiction on the grounds that European integration was an outward-looking, internationalist project while Scottish self-government was an inward – and backward-looking one. In the eyes of the anti-self-government actors – especially business organisations – the very nature of the process of supra-state integration was delegitimising the demand for self-government at sub-state level. The most important determinant of this perception is, again, to be found in the ideological framework with which pro-self-government actors perceived European integration and in the relative positions of the EU and UK political systems in relation to Scotland.

European dimension not exploited

The two factors discussed above led to the pro-self-government actors – again with the exception of the Church of Scotland – not to use the European dimension in their strategies to secure their objectives. The fundamental problem is they could not successfully exploit something they perceived as antithetical to their cause. As the European dimension was not incorporated in their strategies, the self-government game between the pro and anti fronts was played entirely on two levels only – Scotland and the UK. In a purely British dimension, however, the pro-self-government side was at a structural disadvantage vis-à-vis their opponents due to the split between the objectives of devolution and of independence. The demand for independence, perceived as associated with the rise of the SNP, had been the driving force of the whole politics of self-government in Scotland and Labour's policy of devolution had been developed in competition with the Conservatives' preference for the status quo but against the SNP's independence policy. This determined that

conflict intensity was actually higher within the pro-self-government camp
than between the latter and the anti-self-government front. Such conflict
intensity was clearly displayed during the 1979 referendum campaign. The
anti-self-government actors fully exploited the conflict within the pro camp
by exposing their contradictions and by focusing on the links between devolution and secession. It appears that the failure to exploit the European
dimension was due to the weight of mid-to-long-term structural factors
which left next to no margin for manoeuvre to short-term actor agency when
the issue of Scottish self-government took centre-stage. Constrained by their
ideological perspectives on capitalism, democracy and nationalism and by the
entrenched pattern of party competition, the SNP, Labour and the STUC, in
particular, largely failed to grasp that the European dimension was potentially
offering them a 'wild card' in the strategy to achieve self-government.

Mass public

As already seen in chapter 4, elite actors had been effective in shaping public
opinion and in reproducing at mass level the pattern of perceptions, positions
and associations observed at elite level, including the association between
support for self-government and hostility towards the EU. Their failure to
exploit the European dimension, however, prevented them from addressing
some key attitudes at mass level which had the potential to undermine the Yes
vote in the referendum in spite of devolution enjoying majority support. Chief
among them were the deep and widespread hostility to independence, preference for the status quo over independence as 'second best' and the strong
belief that devolution would be a stepping-stone to independence rather than
an antidote to it. The interaction between these attitudes exerted its effects in
the referendum vote and determined the rejection of devolution. The failure
to Europeanise was thus also a failure to influence public opinion enough to
support the elite project of devolution.

Negative perception of the EU

The mirroring of elite attitudes by the mass public was clearly on display
where perceptions of the European Union are concerned. The prevailing attitude was negative but there was significant variation depending on party identification. Labour and Nationalist identifiers were hostile while Liberals and
Conservatives were favourable. This matches the Labour party, the STUC
and the SNP deeply negative position in contrast with the much more positive attitude of the Conservative party, the Liberals and the Church of

Scotland. This pattern appears to have largely been dictated by ideology and social class whereby mainly working-class voters identifying with the Labour party or the SNP viewed European integration as a threat whereas mainly middle-class voters identifying with the Liberals or the Conservatives saw it as an opportunity. This pattern of attitudes determined that, with the partial exception of Liberal identifiers, the demand for self-government was associated with hostility towards the European Union whereas opposition to devolution and independence was associated with support for the EU. It also determined that the pro-self-government camp, again with the exception of the Liberals, perceived the EU as a 'negative extension' of the UK rather than an alternative to it, once again in line with the discourse of the SNP, Labour and the STUC.

Hostility towards independence

A similar mirroring of elite attitudes can be detected with regard to attitudes to independence. As the SNP was 'ostracised' by the UK-wide parties – Labour in particular – likewise the party and its key policy of independence were seen as extreme by the mass public. It is significant that not even a majority of Nationalist identifiers supported secession in 1979. The SNP's position on the European question is likely to have significantly contributed to making the party look extreme and undermining support for its flagship policy. The key consequence of this was that independence was very much feared in the 1970s and that this fear increased as the referendum campaign threw a much sharper light on what independence really was and the consequences it would have for Scotland. This led, crucially, to an almost generalised preference for the status quo over independence among devolutionists. Here again, one sees a clear match with the attitudes and the discourse of Labour and the STUC, in particular, whose support for devolution was directed against the lure of independence more than against the shortcomings of the status quo, on the basis of the tacit assumption that the latter was preferable to the former.

'Interaction effect'

The presence of a link between the two self-government options and the particular shape of the preference distribution between the status quo, devolution and independence produced an 'interaction effect' between attitudes to independence and attitudes to devolution. This has to be understood against the background that, as the whole politics of self-government in Scotland had been driven by the rise of the secessionist SNP, devolution was perceived as being linked to independence and possibly a 'stepping-stone' to the latter. Hostility to independence hence had the 'destructive' effect of undermining the Yes vote in the referendum even though, of course, independence was not as such at stake in the referendum. So much so that a 60 per cent 'virtual' support for self-government turned into a rejection of devolution in the referendum. The effect was particularly powerful among those supporting a 'weaker' form of devolution, i.e. the 'assembly' option, a majority of whom voted No in the referendum. They thought that devolution would lead to independence and they had a much more negative opinion of the latter than of the status quo. They thus found themselves in the uncomfortable position of being in favour of a limited degree of self-government while being acutely aware that that limited degree was highly likely to turn into a maximum degree of self-government, which they thoroughly disliked. If faced with the ultimate choice between status quo and independence, they preferred the status quo. This generated the extraordinary outcome that the Scotland Act 1978 was sunk in the referendum by its core supporters!

Conclusions

Three main conclusions emerge from the analysis conducted so far of the politics of self-government in the 1970s. First, there was a close match between the elites and the mass public. The pattern of attitudes at the elite level was closely mirrored by the pattern of opinions at mass public level. This provides support for the theoretical assumption outlined in chapter 1 that public opinion was shaped by the elites' discourse and campaigning strategies. In other words that elite agency was a crucial intervening variable in determining the dependent variable. It is thus possible to identify a causal mechanism linking perceptions, beliefs and actions at the elite level, distribution of preferences at mass level, voting behaviour in the referendum and, ultimately, the fate of devolution. Secondly, elite actors perceived the European dimension as largely irrelevant for the politics of self-government, and antithetical as far as links were identified. On that basis, they decided, in a narrowly rational way, not to exploit the European dimension to bolster their strategy for or against devolution. This led, thirdly, to the politics of self-government being a 'two-level game' in the 1970s, entirely played within a Scottish–British dimension. Unfortunately for the Scotland Act 1978, pro-self-government actors were at a structural disadvantage – because of their divisions and contradictions – vis-à-vis their opponents within the 'two-level' UK context. The latter successfully exploited their advantage and craftily engineered a rejection of devolution in the referendum. The failure to Europeanise the politics of self-government thus loomed large in the ultimate defeat of devolution in the 1970s.

All the hypothesised effects of the European dimension on the politics of Scottish self-government listed in chapter 1 have thus to be rejected as far as the 1970s are concerned. No Europeanisation took place, hence the null hypothesis holds.

Notes

1 This section also draws on the analysis of the printed media, conducted in Dardanelli (2002: chapter 5).
2 Ibidem.
3 The Liberal party does not fit this description, as it was both pro-European and pro-devolution. However, as explained above, it was not included in the present analysis.

Part II
THE 1990s

6
Political parties

Despite significant change in the Scottish party system between the 1970s and the 1990s, in particular the accelerated decline of the Conservatives and the stabilisation at a fairly high level of the SNP, party positions on self-government remained remarkably stable. Labour championed devolution, the SNP pursued independence but supported devolution as second best and the Conservatives favoured the status quo, albeit this time also in principle as well as in practice. The strategic playing of the self-government game, on the other hand, notably in relation to the European dimension, was in stark contrast to the previous period. By the 1990s, the pro-self-government parties had a positive perception of the European Union, built an explicit European side to their policies and fully exploited the European dimension in their strategies. This was particularly the case for the SNP, which re-centred its strategy around the 'Independence in Europe' position and effectively made secession 'mainstream' and acceptable to both elite and mass opinion. The placing of devolution in a European context and, even more so, the 'mainstreaming' of independence also made possible a rapprochement between Labour and the SNP that gave the pro-side a distinct advantage vis-à-vis their opponents with a far-reaching impact on the referendum outcome.

The Scottish National party

Following a deep crisis immediately after the 1979 referendum and general election, the party went through a phase of renewal and from 1988 onwards began to rise again. It polled 21.5 per cent and won three seats in 1992 and 22.1 per cent and six seats in 1997. By the time of the second referendum, it was the second party in Scotland and the effective opposition to Labour.

Self-government policy

The renewal of the party in the early-to-mid-1980s was based on an effort to 'mainstream' the party and its key policy of independence and make it a credible alternative to the more established parties. A central element of this was a revision of the external context and the procedure for achieving independence. As regards the former, the party went from a commitment to withdraw an independent Scotland from the EU subject to a referendum to making membership the cornerstone of its strategy. By 1988, this led to the adoption of a policy of 'independence in Europe' based on secession from the UK but continued membership of the EU as an additional member state. In relation to independence itself, the party abandoned the implicit automatism of its past positions and, by 1997, committed itself to giving the Scottish people in a referendum the final say.

Despite this effort to moderate the image of the party and to increase the appeal of secession the prospect of achieving independence for Scotland from the constitutional status quo remained a distant one. As in the 1970s, the party was thus facing the dilemma of what policy to adopt towards devolution, hence towards its main proponent, the Labour party. The dilemma was even more acute than in the 1970s as Labour was committed to setting up a Parliament with more extensive self-government competences than the 1970s assembly. Two phases can be identified in the SNP's strategy vis-à-vis Labour's plans. In the first one, during the period 1988–92, the party felt that its new 'independence in Europe' policy would be a vote-winner and expected a breakthrough in the 1992 general election. In this phase, the party maintained a strong opposition to devolution and to the Labour party. The most clear example of this was the refusal to join the Constitutional Convention which was intended to represent the whole spectrum of Scottish society and, in particular, of its demand for self-government. After the disappointing performance in the 1992 general election, the party reconsidered its hostility towards devolution and started to move closer to Labour. As in the 1970s, therefore, the 'gradualist' tendencies within the party prevailed and, despite a small crisis when Labour modified its initial position and announced that the devolution proposals would be put to a referendum, the SNP did not reverse its stance. This eventually led to the party playing a major role in the unified Yes-Yes campaign side by side with Labour, the Liberal Democrats and pro-devolution pressure groups. As in 1979, the party played down any reference to independence in its campaign for the 1997 referendum and adopted the same discourse as the devolutionist actors, advocating the establishment of a Scottish Parliament as a marked improvement on the status quo and as a first exercise of self-government for the country.

Perception and strategic use of the EU

The SNP's perception of the European Union in this period was radically different from that of the 1970s. The party moved from being the one most opposed to European integration to being, in certain respects, the one most in favour of it, though some divisions within the party remained. As mentioned above, by 1988 not only had the party fully accepted Scotland's membership of the European Union but it had turned it into the cornerstone of its independence policy. This was based on an overall positive perception of the European Union in general and of its effect on Scotland in particular, though some of the old doubts lingered on. The party still harboured some concerns about Scotland's peripherality but overall it saw the single market as being positive for Scotland. Likewise, it also maintained reservations about the EU decision-making process and the agricultural and fisheries policies but these were placed within an overall positive framework perceiving the EU as a progressive supra-state political system in which small nations and regions could play a full part. In particular, in this period the SNP was explicitly comparing the European 'union' with the British 'union' and perceived the former as a 'positive alternative' to the latter, for it displayed different and more desirable characteristics. Above all, as explained below, in the 1990s the SNP perceived the European Union as a political system facilitating the achievement of the party's goal of Scottish independence whereas in the 1970s the EU was seen as placing additional constraints.

A number of factors determined this radical change in attitudes towards the EU. As discussed at greater length in chapter 10, they included the inflow of foreign direct investments and structural funds money into Scotland and the development of a social dimension to EU policies. These positive developments were seen as outweighing the still unpopular aspects such as the fisheries policy.[1] They also included significant changes within the party itself, both in terms of ideology and personnel. National sovereignty ceased to be conceptualised as a monolithic, zero-sum entity and the idea that it could be pooled or vertically segmented without relinquishing it became widely accepted. A less interventionist and protectionist economic policy was widely embraced which helped in reconciling the party with the EU's 'economic constitution'. As regards the latter aspect, a new generation of leaders took control of the party and were instrumental in changing attitudes towards the EU. This was despite the fact that some of them had previously been deeply hostile to it. Winnie Ewing and Jim Sillars, in particular, played a key role in this 'conversion'.[2]

On this positive perception of the EU, the SNP built a new policy of seeking secession from the UK but placing an independent Scotland firmly in the context of EU membership, under the slogan of 'independence in Europe'.[3] The 'independence in Europe' policy was explicitly intended to take advantage of the incentives and opportunities that the EU system was offering in order to increase the appeal of independence – hence of the SNP – at mass public level. In Gordon Wilson's, the party's leader in the 1980s, words, 'I wanted to make it easier for people to vote for the SNP and for independence [and] I saw Europe as a counterweight to London'.[4] In the party's discourse, the European Union was portrayed as a confederal union of independent member states and contrasted with a unitary, centralised UK state with the obvious claim that the former was providing a much more favourable framework for Scotland than the latter. According to the party's spokesman, Kevin Pringle, 'the whole concept of a small country in Europe has become a powerful argument for us . . . Europe is a powerful campaigning tool for the SNP'.[5] More particularly, the SNP claimed that 'independence in Europe' would remove the charge of separatism, would eliminate the economic costs of secession and would increase Scotland's influence on policy-making at the Union level.

These claims rested on three properties of the EU political system that constituted opportunities and incentives for independence in the eyes of the SNP. At a general level, the insertion of independence within the process of European integration intended to transcend the nation-states removed the negative connotation of secession, such as the ideas of separation and isolation. The European framework thus offered the opportunity to reduce the symbolic costs of secession.[6] The second opportunity offered was in the economic sphere. Here the key factor was that the existence of an EU-wide customs union and the development of the single market offered the guarantee that an independent Scotland within the EU would retain full access to the English market. The potential loss of the English market for companies operating in an independent Scotland had always been the main economic cost of independence and a stumbling block in broadening its appeal beyond the committed hard core. In Gordon Wilson's words at the 1983 conference, this aspect made the new policy a 'first class way of pushing the advantages of political independence without any threat of economic dislocation'.[7] The party was acutely aware that for independence ever to receive majority support, the economic consequences had to be clearly addressed and the party had to be deemed capable of governing the country, as the lessons of the 1979 defeat and of the subsequent decline of support showed.[8] Lastly, but most importantly, the party exploited the fact that the institutional structure of the EU over-represented the interests of the small countries vis-à-vis the larger states, to argue that the European union would be a much more favourable political framework for Scotland than the British Union.[9] Crucial in this respect was the party's ability to claim that only member-state status would give adequate representation at the Union level when the latter was becoming increasingly important with the development of the process of integration and the Conservative party's self-inflicted isolation reducing the UK political influence within the Council of Ministers. As the manifesto for the 1994 European election put it, 'Scotland needs to change . . . central to that change is the need for a powerful, direct voice in Europe. An independent Scotland sitting at the top table beside the other nations of Europe will totally change our situation'.[10] In Pringle's words, 'as the Union level acquires more and more policy-making competences, it becomes ever more important for Scotland to 'maximise its voice at the European level'.[11]

It should come as no surprise that in its pro-EU discourse the party ignored the fact that automatic EU membership for a seceding Scotland was far from assured and that the process of integration itself had the potential to run counter to nationalist aspirations. If, on the one hand, the EU was lowering the economic, political and symbolic costs of secession it was also threatening the very national sovereignty that the party wanted to achieve for Scotland.[12] The 'independence in Europe' policy can thus be seen as a strategic gamble on the part of the SNP to trade more certain short-term 'office' gains against uncertain long-term 'policy' pay-offs. In other words, embracing European integration to facilitate accession to independence, betting that the process of integration would not go as far as rendering such independence meaningless.

The Labour party

Labour increased its already dominant position in Scotland from the 1970s to the 1990s leading to a tally of 56 seats and 45.6 per cent of the vote in the 1997 general election.[13]

Self-government policy

Despite the results of the referendum and of the general election of 1979, and the subsequent decline of the SNP, Labour maintained a commitment to a directly elected assembly in both the 1983 and 1987 general elections, though the issue remained at a low level of saliency. From 1988 onwards, however, under the impulse of the Scottish party, a qualitative change took place in Labour's position on self-government. The crucial step was the decision, under the leadership of Donald Dewar, to take part in the Scottish Constitutional Convention with the aim of arriving at a set of proposals acceptable to a broad range of the pro-devolution actors in Scotland and which the party would commit itself to implement once in office. Over the years 1989–90, Scottish Labour played a major part in the Convention's work and when the latter published its report in 1990 the party adopted its proposals as official policy. The Convention's report called for the establishment of a Scottish Parliament elected by proportional representation and with significant economic and some fiscal powers. In the Scottish manifesto for the 1992 general election the party declared that it 'will immediately introduce legislation to establish an elected Scottish Parliament. Labour's legislation will be firmly based on the proposals agreed in the Scottish Constitutional Convention'.[14] It also stressed that devolution would be more than a purely symbolic move as the Parliament would have extensive legislative powers and the ability to represent Scotland at UK and EU level.[15] Despite the defeat in that election the party's stance was reinforced by the accession of John Smith to the leadership of the UK party. A Scotsman and a long-time supporter of devolution, he considered devolution to be the 'settled will of the Scottish people'.[16] After Smith's death, Tony Blair continued the same policy, endorsing the second report of the Constitutional Convention, presented in 1995. The party then decided to put the issue to a referendum after the general election with the later change of having two questions, one on establishing the Parliament and the other on granting it tax-varying powers. Once the party triumphed in the May 1997 election it promptly moved to hold a referendum on 11 September. Throughout this period, the party remained opposed to independence and kept portraying it in negative terms as a policy bringing political isolation, economic damage and social disruption to Scotland, though with much less hostility towards it than in the 1970s.

As Deacon has pointed out, 'the party's conversion to, and eventual participation in, the Scottish Constitutional Convention marked a watershed in its attitude to the question of Scottish Home Rule'.[17] This was so for three main reasons. First, Labour subscribed to a degree of self-government far greater than the one previously endorsed by the party, still largely based on the Scotland Act 1978, including in particular, significant economic and fiscal powers. Second, due to the compromise the party had to reach with the Liberal Democrats in order to retain the latter's co-operation in the Convention, Labour had to accept the principle of an electoral system for the Scottish Parliament based on proportional representation which would thus reduce its ability to exercise control of the body. Last, but most importantly, the party accepted the principle laid out in the 1988 Claim of Right, namely that, as far as the Scottish nation was concerned, sovereignty rested with the Scottish people rather than with the Westminster Parliament. It thus put loyalty to Scotland before loyalty to the UK.[18] The decision to join the Convention can be seen as a move by which the party was prepared to pay a price in terms of freedom of manoeuvre and control of the future assembly in exchange for strengthening the credibility of its devolution policy by 'institutionalising' it.[19]

Three main factors explain the Labour party's commitment to the Convention and to a higher degree of self-government than in 1979. First, the ideological revision that the party underwent throughout the 1980s and the early 1990s, which resulted in the abandonment of the belief in government-led management of the economy – which required state centralisation – and in the endorsement of 'new growth' theories in which regional governments played an important role.[20] Second, the attempt by the Conservative government to impose on Scotland policies that were clearly unpopular. The case of the poll tax, further exacerbated by the fact that it was introduced in Scotland one year ahead of England, was the most glaring example.[21] Combined with the continuous erosion of the Conservative vote north of the border, this created a 'democratic deficit' that the Labour party was willing to exploit. Third, but most importantly, the SNP's change of policy, which threatened to make 'independence in Europe' the main alternative to the status quo thus hollowing out the self-government centre-ground represented by devolution.[22]

The party's discourse on self-government was still largely based on the 1970s arguments but with emphasis on three new elements. First, as already discussed, the fundamental assumption was that within the Scottish political system, sovereignty ultimately rested with the Scottish people rather than the Westminster Parliament. Second, there was greater emphasis on the fact that the democratic deficit created by the minority Conservative rule made the need to democratise the Scottish Office even more necessary and urgent than in the past. Closely linked to this point was the claim that devolution would result in marked improvement of public services which were undermined by the Conservatives' policies. Lastly, as discussed below, there was much more emphasis on the European dimension and on the role the proposed Parliament would be able to play in that dimension.

Two other aspects of Labour's policy were also significantly different from the 1970s. First, the party was much more united behind the official policy on devolution, though a small minority around Tam Dalyell continued their crusade against it. Secondly, the relationship with the SNP changed sharply. By then the party perceived its policy of devolution to be directed primarily against the Conservative party and the status quo rather than the SNP. In this light, the SNP was rather an ally in the common battle against the status quo. This led to the decision to conduct a unified Yes-Yes campaign group with the SNP and the Liberal Democrats for the 1997 referendum. The rapprochement between the two parties was based on a careful playing down of the differences on independence which had been so much at the forefront

eighteen years earlier and clearly on a radical transformation of the public perception of independence in comparison with 1979. Remarkably, this playing
down took place despite the fact that the No side – including Tam Dalyell –
still centred their discourse on the link between devolution and secession.[23]

Perception and strategic use of the EU

Since the mid-1980s, Labour's perception of the EU underwent a profound
transformation which moved the party from a commitment to withdrawal to
strong support for membership and, to a lesser extent, for further integration. By the mid-1990s the Labour party was much more pro-EU than ever
before and also more pro-EU than the Conservatives. It had developed a
positive attitude to economic integration in general and to the latter's impact
on Scotland in particular. The ideological revision within Labour meant that
economic integration no longer conflicted with the party's economic policies
while evidence accumulated that Scotland was thriving within the single
market. The change in perception had been made easier by the fact that the
EU started to develop social and regional policies whose objectives had
always been at the heart of the party's principles and beliefs while these were
being phased out or undermined in the Conservative-ruled UK. More generally, the Labour party in Scotland thus came to see the EU as a progressive,
multi-level political system which was a necessary response to the challenges
of the late twentieth century such as economic globalisation, security threats
and environmental problems. This progressive system was favourably contrasted with a constitutionally archaic and socially regressive Conservative-
ruled UK state. Like the SNP, the Labour party was thus also seeing the EU
as a 'positive alternative' to the UK and, moreover, as a facilitator of the
demand for devolution.[24]

On this changed perception of the European Union, the Labour party
built a European dimension to its devolution policy with the objective of coun-
teracting the competitive challenge represented by the SNP's decision to fully
exploit the EU to boost support for independence. The focus of the party's
policy was to demonstrate that devolution was the best constitutional option
for Scotland not only within the UK but within the wider EU as well. This was
directed at countering the SNP's claim that only 'independence in Europe'
would maximise Scotland's influence at the Union level. The argument was
fully spelt out in the party's submission to the Scottish Constitutional
Convention on the European dimension to devolution.[25] Authored by David
Martin, MEP for the Lothians and de facto leader of Labour Scottish MEPs,
the document stressed the crucial importance of the European dimension for
Scotland and the vital need to maximise the representation of its interests in

'Brussels'.[26] In order to achieve this objective it proposed the establishment of a Scottish European office in Brussels and it advocated for a post-devolution Scotland the same type of representation enjoyed by the German regions, described as 'the maximum possible representation within the EC for a non-member state'.[27] These proposals were placed in a framework of strong support for a 'Europe of the Regions' scenario that went as far as supporting 'the establishment of a second elected chamber of the Regions which would eventually replace the Council of Ministers'.[28] Martin's proposals became the official policy of the Scottish Labour party even though his radicalism in favour of a 'Europe of the Regions' was toned down into a less controversial support for the Committee of the Regions established by the Maastricht Treaty. In the 1992 election manifesto the Scottish party stated: 'Labour is determined to give Scotland a place at the centre of European affairs. As part of Scotland's evolving role in Europe, we will establish a representative office in Brussels and seek appropriate representation for Scotland in European institutions'.[29] The European dimension of devolution was played down in the 1997 general election manifesto which had very much a British rather than a Scottish focus, though reference was made to the relevance of the principle of subsidiarity for the distribution of power within the UK,[30] but was prominent again in the campaign for the devolution referendum. The 'Yes-Yes' leaflet produced by the Scottish Labour MEPs claimed: 'A Scottish Parliament would be the most efficient, the most effective, the most democratic and the natural channel for Scottish participation in European Union programmes and organisations'.[31] In sum, the Labour party claimed that devolution would result in a 'best of both worlds' situation, as it would allow Scotland to retain access to the political resources of the UK while at the same time acquiring the ability to represent specific Scottish interests, in contrast to the 'extremist' defence of the status quo, and an independence policy 'out of touch with European developments'.[32] More particularly, the status quo was attacked on the grounds that it did not provide a satisfactory representation of Scotland's interests in the EU while independence was deemed to be highly costly in economic, political and 'affective' terms.[33]

Labour's claim that devolution would grant Scotland more influence within the EU than either the status quo or independence rested on three main arguments. First, it utilised the fact that European integration was posing growing constraints on state governments' economic policy to claim that governmental capabilities at regional level were an increasingly crucial factor of economic competitiveness.[34] Secondly, the decision to establish a Committee of the Regions to give regional governments more influence in EU policy-making risked further marginalising Scotland without a unitary representation.[35] The idea of a 'Europe of the Regions', the European-wide trend towards regionalisation and, especially, the adoption of the principle of subsidiarity – together with the long-standing anti-nationalist element of the rhetoric of European integration – were also exploited to give devolution a normative justification as a progressive policy vis-à-vis secession and the status quo and thus undermine the Nationalist and Conservative policies. The third, but most important argument was that the increased importance of policy-making at the EU level made more necessary a direct representation of Scottish interests in the EU but that this would be maximised by acting within the UK framework.[36]

In this period the Labour party thus clearly saw the EU as facilitating its devolution policy by providing incentives and opportunities for the establishment of regional government. It is worth pointing out, though, that not everyone in the party was seeing the EU as a facilitator of devolution. In his anti-devolution discourse the veteran No campaigner Tam Dalyell linked devolution to independence and the latter to a weakening of Scotland's influence: 'it seems to me that what you are proposing [is] to take Scotland on the road to independence which many indeed may want but it is at the price of real power and influence in Britain and Europe'.[37]

The Conservative party

The party declined quite dramatically between 1979 and 1997, from being the second party in Scotland to the fourth place. In 1997, it attracted less than 20 per cent of the votes and lost all its MPs.[38]

Self-government policy

The party's hostility to Scottish self-government developed in 1976–79 was greatly reinforced by the referendum result and became entrenched during the long years of the Thatcher governments. The party abandoned the distinction between opposition to an assembly along the lines of the Scotland Act 1978 but support for the principle of devolution and adopted a position of complete rejection of self-government. For most of the 1980s, however, the issue of self-government was virtually removed from the centre-stage of party competition despite the fact that the continuous erosion of support for the Conservatives in Scotland was attributed by many to their position on self-government. From 1988 onwards, as seen above, the party faced a renewed challenge from a modernised Labour party and a resurgent SNP and their revised policies on self-government. The Conservatives' response was to retrench into a dogged defence of the status quo, to refuse to join the

Constitutional Convention and to fight the 1992 and 1997 general elections and the 1997 referendum campaign on a platform of total opposition to devolution. The change of leadership between Margaret Thatcher and John Major in 1990 had no visible effect on the party's position. This radicalisation of the position on self-government isolated the Conservatives within Scottish society and, coupled with the low profile adopted by the business organisations, led to the party fighting the No-No corner of the 1997 referendum campaign in almost complete isolation.[39]

Three factors appear to have shaped the evolution of the Conservative position into a strenuous and almost dogmatic defence of the status quo. First, the prospect of the SNP becoming the dominant force in Scotland and a serious electoral threat to the party, which seemed close enough after the October 1974 election, failed to materialise and the Conservatives did not believe that the 'independence in Europe' policy would reverse the trend. The party was convinced that between the status quo and independence – even within the EU – the Scots would always choose the former. Second, the party interpreted the 1979 referendum result as a clear indication that the Scots did not want a devolved assembly which threatened to put the union with England at risk. Furthermore, they interpreted it as signalling the existence of a large gap between the elites and the ordinary people. Lastly, but probably more importantly, the Thatcherite 'revolution' had turned the Conservatives into a party ideologically committed to a minimal role of government in society. Combined with the traditional Conservative belief in unionism, this ruled out any form of Scottish self-government, as the latter would have meant adding an extra layer of government and bureaucracy and putting the unity of the UK at risk. In Thatcher's words, the party's interpretation of the principle of bringing government closer to the people was by 'rolling back the state rather than creating new institutions of governance'.[40] The Scottish party fully shared this view and was more united behind it than in 1979.

In a similar guise as in 1979, the party concentrated its discourse against devolution on two main arguments. The first was the long-standing claim that devolution would bring unnecessary extra government and extra costs with the additional threat this time of higher taxation. This was, of course, a consequence of the fact that the Parliament proposed by the Constitutional Convention and adopted by the Labour party had more power – notably a limited tax-varying power – than the 1979 assembly. In the Conservatives' rhetoric, the body was no longer simply 'redundant' but it had become clearly 'dangerous' for ordinary citizens in general and for economic actors in particular. The costs of devolution – leaving the spectre of secession apart – would thus derive mainly from higher taxation that would put Scottish households and businesses at a disadvantage relative to their counterparts in

England rather than from the costs of extra politicians and extra bureaucrats as such. The proposed Parliament's tax-varying powers, dubbed the 'tartan tax' by the Conservatives, became, especially through the interventions of the Scottish leader Forsyth, one of the main issues in the campaign.[41]

The central plank of the party's argument, however, was, as in 1979, that devolution was the first step towards the break-up of the UK. It had to be opposed because secession was not in Scotland's interests, either politically or economically. Such an argument was widely used in the campaigns for the three main contests that took place in this period. In 1992, John Major warned that Labour's devolution policy was putting the United Kingdom 'in danger'[42] while five years later he wrote in the party's Scottish manifesto that 'the menace of separatism – introduced through the Trojan Horse of devolution – would blight the lives of Scots for generations to come'.[43] In the same election manifesto, the Scottish leader of the party, Michael Forsyth, warned against 'separatist policies whose consequences would be to detach us from the United Kingdom and impoverish our people for generations to come'.[44] In the crucial phase of the 1997 referendum campaign, Michael Ancram, the party's constitutional spokesman and leader of the *Think Twice* group, argued that 'within ten years, you would see an enormous cesspool of resentment build up which can only play into the hands of nationalism and the separatist movement'.[45]

The first line of attack – on the 'tartan tax' – had a limited success. It arguably forced the Labour government to change its mind and put two questions on the referendum ballot and was probably instrumental in delivering lower support for tax-varying powers than for the principle of devolution itself, though it did not stop these powers from being endorsed. In contrast, the main line of attack centred on the break-up of the UK totally failed to produce the outcome the No side achieved in 1979. Support for devolution held steady throughout the campaign and turned into a large Yes vote in the referendum.

Perception and strategic use of the EU

The Conservatives' attitudes towards the EU moved in the opposite direction to those of Labour and the SNP. The Conservatives went from being the 'party of Europe' in the 1970s to being the 'Eurosceptical' party in the 1990s. Though the Conservative government supported the single-market programme and ratified the Maastricht treaty, its dominant perception of the EU had turned negative. More specifically, the party retained a positive perception of economic integration based on free trade and market liberalisation – hence support for the single-market programme – but turned hostile to the political aspects of increased supra-nationalism and, especially, of adding a 'social dimension' to the integration process. The bottom line had been set by Margaret Thatcher in her famous Bruges speech in 1988 when she declared that the party had 'not successfully rolled back the frontiers of the state in Britain only to see them reimposed at a European level'.[46] Accordingly, the party strongly opposed the Social Charter of the Maastricht treaty and monetary union and eventually negotiated opt-out clauses from both. Together with the traditional concern of preserving UK's sovereignty, there is substantial evidence that it was precisely the development of a 'social Europe' that turned the party against the European Union.[47]

In this light, it is possible to appreciate how the decision on the part of the SNP and Labour to exploit the European dimension to strengthen the case for self-government represented a serious competitive challenge for the party. Its rivals had opened a new dimension to the politics of Scottish self-government in which the Conservatives – given their negative attitude towards Europe – were at a structural disadvantage. The party reacted to this challenge by accepting to compete in the European dimension as well and by trying to turn it to its advantage. Its strategy rested on the exploitation of three arguments.

First, the party used Europe as a rhetorical device to place a Conservative-governed Scotland in a positive international framework, and to defend the party's record on the pursuit of Scottish interests within the EU, particularly from an economic point of view. This was clearly on display in the 1997 general election manifesto, which put Scotland firmly into a European framework rather than a purely British one.[48] From this position, the party was able to attack Labour's claim that a devolved government was necessary to boost Scotland competitiveness, on the ground that the direct and indirect extra costs generated by the creation of devolved institutions were much greater than the gains to be obtained through government policies in the economic sphere. Therefore, the acquisition of self-government would have the effect of worsening Scotland's competitive position vis-à-vis other European regions and to damage Scotland's economy.[49] Second, the Conservatives added a European element to the claim that devolution would fatally weaken the UK: devolution and European integration were two faces of the same process of 'power draining away from Westminster'.[50] Lastly, the party argued that the political nature of the EU and the prospect of enlargement reinforced the case against self-government on the grounds that only through the political power and influence of the UK government could Scottish interests be defended at the European level. As the manifesto for the 1992 general election put it, 'Scotland's voice [in the EU] will be weakened by the creation of a separate Scottish Parliament'.[51]

In sum, the Conservative party perceived the European Union as placing constraints on self-government for Scotland and tried to turn this into an argument reinforcing the case for the retention of the status quo. However, as mentioned above, this was a difficult argument to make, given the party's negative stance towards the EU and, more specifically, the fact that the self-inflicted isolation of the Conservative-ruled UK was hard to reconcile with the claim that the status quo maximised Scotland's influence in Europe. As it turned out, the gamble was unsuccessful as the party failed to persuade the electorate that its interpretation of what European integration meant for Scotland was the best one.

Conclusions

As the evidence analysed in this chapter shows, the European dimension was crucial to party competition on self-government over the period 1988–97. Parties clearly identified several connections between the European Union and the issue of self-government for Scotland and understood them as either providing opportunities/incentives or placing constraints on the latter. On that basis, they incorporated a European dimension into their positions on self-government. The SNP was the key actor in this dynamic: it was the party that exploited the European Union to its fullest and by so doing effectively opened an additional dimension in the politics of self-government. The SNP move forced the other parties to also play the self-government game in a European dimension.

This extra-dimension had a double effect. First, it strengthened the pro-self-government side – Labour and the SNP – vis-à-vis the Conservatives by moving the battle onto a terrain that was structurally disadvantageous for the latter. By so doing it also acted as a factor of unity within the self-government side despite some lingering conflict between the two main actors. Second, within this pro-self-government side, by making independence mainstream and raising support for it, it strengthened the position of the SNP, making it a more dangerous rival to the Labour party but also an indispensable partner in the battle against the status quo. The rapprochement between Labour and the SNP can thus be explained by the fact that the former's position was by then closer to the latter's than to the Conservatives'. This shift was produced by the competitive dynamics unleashed by the SNP's move to the centre implicit in its decision to place independence in the context of the EU. The SNP's move shifted the preference distribution at public level towards the 'independence in Europe' option and threatened to polarise competition between the latter and the status quo leaving the assembly option looking like an 'empty centre'.[52] The Labour move can thus be seen as an attempt to move as close as possible to the SNP's position, in order to regain the centre-ground, without going beyond the party's 'region of acceptability'. The reduction of the policy gap between Labour and the SNP was crucial in making possible a united Yes campaign in the 1997 referendum.[53]

Within this new European dimension, competition between parties focused on which one of the three constitutional statuses for Scotland was best able to meet three requirements. First, to be most in tune with the process of European integration. This was an attempt by the competing parties to claim a European legitimacy for their respective policies. Second, to provide the best institutional framework for developing Scotland's competitiveness within the single European market. Third, to maximise the representation of Scottish interests at the Union level in terms of both effectiveness and democratic accountability. Across the three issues, the pro-self-government arguments enjoyed higher coherence and credibility. Hence, exploitation of the European dimension gave the pro-self-government actors a structural advantage that they utilised to secure the endorsement of a Scottish Parliament in the 1997 referendum.

Notes

1 Cunningham, interview with the author.
2 See wider discussion in Dardanelli (2002: 112–13).
3 On the adoption of the 'independence in Europe' policy, see Macartney (1990), Lynch (1996: 37–49) and Ichijo (2004: esp. 43–58).
4 Interview with the author; also Cunningham, interview with the author.
5 Interview with the author. See also *SNPower for Change*, pp. 4 and 8–9.
6 See Sillars (1986: 182).
7 Quoted in Lynch (1996: 38). See also Sillars (1986: 184–6) and *SNPower for Change*, pp. 6–7.
8 See Sillars (1986: 182).
9 Small countries are on an equal footing with larger ones in terms of presidency of the Council and the right of veto and over-represented in the power of appointing commissioners, in the voting weights in the Council and in the share of seats in the Parliament.
10 *SNPower for Change*, p. 2.
11 Interview with the author. Also, Wilson and Wolfe, interviews with the author.
12 On the legal problems raised by a seceding Scotland with regard to EU membership, see Lane (1991) and Murkens (2002). For an articulate internal critique of the 'independence in Europe' policy, see Lindsay (1991). Even those in favour of the policy are fully aware of the existence of such a trade-off, Wilson and Cunningham, interviews with the author; see also *SNPower for Change*, p. 19 and Lynch (1996).

13 On electoral support for the Labour party in Scotland, see Bennie et al. (1997: 50).
14 *Labour Party's Scottish Manifesto* 1992, p. 6.
15 Ibidem.
16 Quoted in Wright (1997: 143).
17 Deacon (1990: 62).
18 On the importance of this step, see Geekie and Levy (1989: especially 400–2) and Mitchell (1998: 489–91).
19 On the latter point, see Bennie et al. (1997: 160).
20 On the ideological transformation of the party, see Mitchell (1998: 479).
21 On the poll tax in Scotland, see McCrone (1991) and Barker (1992).
22 See Geekie and Levy (1989: 409) and Deacon (1990: 70).
23 See 'Connery Says "Yesh, Yesh" to Role in Devolution Adventure', *The Scotsman*, 25 August 1997, and 'Dalyell Warns of One-way Road to Independence', *The Scotsman*, 8 September 1997.
24 On this point, see also Paterson (1994: 4).
25 Submission to the Constitutional Convention, 30 August 1989, Scottish Labour Party archive, TD1384/13.
26 Ibidem.
27 Ibidem.
28 Ibidem; see also Martin (1992).
29 *Scottish Labour 1992 manifesto*, page 23 see also 'A Modern Scotland', p. 8, Scottish Labour Party archive, TD1384/13.
30 *Because Scotland Deserves Better*, p. 32.
31 It also pointed out that 'the strength of the German economy owes much to the federal structure of its government, banks and finance', National Library of Scotland archives, QP4.200.1870.
32 'A Modern Scotland', p. 8; see also *Action for Scotland in Europe*, p. 2 and Millan, interview with the author.
33 'A Modern Scotland', p. 8.
34 Ibidem; also Millan, interview with the author.
35 'A Modern Scotland', p. 8.
36 Ibidem; see also *Action for Scotland in Europe*, p. 1.
37 'McLeish Tries to Appease Dalyell', *Scotland on Sunday*, 17 August 1997.
38 On the decline of the Scottish Conservative party see Kendrick and McCrone (1989) and Seawright (1999).
39 See McCrone and Lewis (1999: 24).
40 Thatcher (1993: 36).
41 See Bennie et al. (1997: 72).
42 Ibidem: 71.
43 *Fighting for Scotland*, p. 2.
44 Ibidem, p. 4.
45 'Tory Attack "Drags Home Rule Debate into Gutter" ', *The Scotsman*, 28 August 1997; see also 'Don't Wreck the Heritage We All Share', by Margaret Thatcher, *The Scotsman*, 9 September 1997.
46 Reproduced in Weigall and Stirk (1992: 180).
47 See Garry (1995: especially 175), Morris (1996: 131–5) and Sowemimo (1996: especially 91–2).

48 *Fighting for Scotland*, p. 9. See also *The Best Future for Scotland*, p. 3.

49 Hutton, interview with the author.

50 ' "72 Hours Left to Save UK", says Major', *The Times*, 29 April 1997; on the link between devolution and secession see also the *Think Twice* campaign literature at the National Library of Scotland archives, QP4.200.1867.

51 See *The Best Future for Scotland*, p. 49; see also *A Strong Britain in a Strong Europe*, pp. 8–10, *Fighting for Scotland*, pp. 38–9 and 47 and Hutton, interview with the author.

52 It should be noted, though, that the SNP was more successful in raising support for independence than in attracting votes for itself.

53 See McCrone and Lewis (1999: 27).

7
Interest groups

Among interest groups as well, the politics of self-government was played differently than in the 1970s, especially in relation to the European dimension. While the Church of Scotland had been isolated in the 1970s in being both pro-devolution and pro-EU and in seeing the latter strengthening the case for the former, it was by then in good company. The key change, of course, concerned the STUC which was in the 1990s one of they key actors in the effort to Europeanise Scottish devolution. Like Labour and the SNP, the STUC's perception of the EU changed radically from deep hostility to a strongly positive view. A second important change between the two periods, which increased the interest groups' influence on the politics of self-government, was the presence of the Constitutional Convention. Although not strictly speaking an interest group – as it included parties, local governments etc. – its role was de facto such that prominent groups such as the Church of Scotland and the STUC used the Convention to maximise their influence on parties, media and public opinion. The exploitation of the European dimension featured prominently in the discourse and campaigning of both the individual interest groups and the Convention. In further contrast with the 1970s, the business associations remained opposed to devolution but felt much less strongly about it, decided to remain on the sidelines of the debate and virtually did not take part in the 1997 referendum campaign. This significantly contributed to weakening the No side in the referendum both financially and presentationally.

The Church of Scotland

Despite increasing secularisation, the Church of Scotland retained an influential voice in Scottish society.[1] Together with the other churches, it took a prominent role in the Constitutional Convention, with the appointment of key members to the Convention's executive committee, and put forward a largely united line on the constitutional question. Both on its own and through the Convention, the Church of Scotland thus continued to be a key player in the politics of self-government.

Self-government policy

In this period the Church's position on self-government had three significant aspects. First, the Church maintained its traditional positions of supporting the establishment of a devolved Parliament and opposing secession. Secondly, the Church took the decision to join the Constitutional Convention and to commit itself to supporting the Convention's proposals for a devolved Scottish Parliament. In the period 1989–95, the Church thus acted primarily through the forum of the Convention and left to the latter the formulation of the details of a desirable devolution scheme. Third, and in contrast with the 1970s, the Church tried to base its position on self-government on theological arguments rather than simply on a vague support for the aspirations of the Scottish nation.[2] This was done in the 1989 report of the Church and Nation committee. The document made two main points. First, that the Church was entitled to take a position on the issue of self-government on the ground of 'its own representative role as a national institution responsive to Scottish opinion and responsible for the nation's moral and spiritual well-being'.[3] Secondly, the Church stated that the demand for self-government in Scotland rested primarily on dissatisfaction with the British constitutional principle of parliamentary sovereignty and on the policies legitimised by that principle. Such a principle was only nominally British for it was entirely based on an English constitutional tradition alien to Scotland. The Scottish tradition had always been one of limited power and popular sovereignty. As a result, 'from a Scottish constitutional and theological perspective this English constitutional tradition of state absolutism has always been unacceptable in theory. It is now intolerable in practice'.[4] The Church thus asserted that sovereignty within the Scottish political system rested with the people of Scotland and that the latter were entitled to decide the form of government that they preferred. Without prescribing one constitutional option over the others, the Church made clear that the Scottish people should be given the opportunity to take such a decision. In this regard, the Church softened even further its opposition to independence and was by then seeing it as a feasible option for Scotland, while officially still being opposed to it. As the Church's spokesman at the presentation of the 1995 report of the Constitutional Convention put it, 'the ultimate outcome of the implementation of the Convention's scheme might well be complete independence'.[5]

Although the Church did not take an active part in the referendum campaign, its influence was arguably greater than in the 1970s, when it was divided and ultimately unable to take an official stand. Through the 'magnifier' of the Convention, the Church's voice on self-government was more influential in the politics of self-government in the 1990s than twenty years earlier.

Perception and strategic use of the EU

The Church of Scotland's attitudes towards the European Union were even more positive in this period than in the 1970s, both as regards the EU itself and Scotland's experience of it, though some concerns about peripherality lingered on. The Church re-affirmed its strong support for what it saw as the fundamental mission of the EU, to end rivalries among the European states and to build an ever-closer union in Europe, and it pointed out that the process of European integration should not be confined to the marketplace. It supported further integration and the democratisation of the EU institutional structures along federalist lines and on the basis of the principle of subsidiarity.

With regard to Scotland's position within the integrating European Union, the Church was still concerned in the late 1980s that Scotland's would be disadvantaged by the completion of the single market due to its peripheral location.[6] To counter the centripetal effects of economic integration and soften the economic and social costs borne by weaker areas, it strongly advocated the development of social and regional policies at the Union level.[7] However, by 1996 the Church had modified its perception and expressed satisfaction with the benefits deriving from social and regional policies and from inward investments.[8] By the time of the second referendum, the Church's positive perception of the effects of economic integration and strong support for social and regional policies were well established.

The Church's use of the European dimension to strengthen the case for self-government was broadly similar to that of the 1970s, with three main aspects. First, sovereignty had to be re-interpreted in a developing European context and self-government was necessary to allow Scotland to play a full part in the emerging multi-level EU system.[9] Secondly, self-government was necessary in order for Scotland's interests to be adequately represented at the Union level. In the Church's view, the deepening of integration represented by the single market programme only made the need for such representation stronger.[10] Lastly, but most importantly, the Church used the European dimension to enhance the legitimacy of its – and Scotland's – demand for self-government on the grounds that the establishment of a Scottish Parliament would be an instance of devolution of power and of application of the principle of subsidiarity and would thus be fully in line with the progressive political trend in Europe. The importance of the European dimension as a legitimating context for the demand for self-government is demonstrated by the fact that the leading critic of the pro-devolution position of the Church also appealed to the European dimension, albeit to point out that the demand for self-government in Scotland was running counter to the process and the spirit of European integration.[11]

The Scottish Trades Union Congress

Two contrasting developments marked the role of the STUC in the politics of devolution in relation to the 1970s. On the one hand, the Congress was weakened by a reduction in membership, the wider process of de-unionisation of the workforce and the hostile attitude towards the trades unions adopted by the Conservative party at both the UK and the Scottish levels. On the other hand, these circumstances, the latter in particular, strengthened the STUC's position as both a 'national' and a 'class' body resisting the Conservative assault on the interests of Scotland's working classes.

Self-government policy

The STUC decided to exploit those circumstances to the full by building broad 'issue coalitions' of interest groups which could claim to demand self-government on behalf of Scottish civil society. It did so by joining the Constitutional Convention and by setting up a campaigning tool called 'Coalition for Scottish Democracy'. As Aitken put it, the STUC became in this period, even more so than in the 1970s, the 'choirmaster of Scottish discontent'.[12] Campbell Christie, the general secretary over the period 1986–98, played a crucial role by becoming a very visible and popular public face at once of the STUC and of the wider pro-devolution front. On his appointment, he declared that his primary objective was to 'help shape a Scottish Parliament'.[13] When the Labour party announced that the devolution proposals would be put to a referendum, the STUC took the view that a referendum was unnecessary but nonetheless committed itself to mobilise its campaigning resources in order to ensure the highest possible Yes vote.[14]

Like the Church of Scotland, the STUC also chose to reaffirm its strong support for the principle of devolution, leaving the formulation and the endorsement of specific proposals to the Constitutional Convention. Its official position was of strong support for the Convention's proposals and for the Labour party's commitment to implement them within one year of gaining office.[15] The Congress also deeply changed its attitudes towards independence, now seen as a feasible though not the best option for Scotland, and towards the SNP, now considered a precious ally in building a broad pro-self-government 'coalition'.[16] Significantly, as detailed below, in supporting devolution rather than independence as the best constitutional status, the STUC chose to emphasise the emotional aspects of the links between Scotland and England rather than the economic costs of secession.

The main drivers of the STUC's support for self-government were also broadly similar to those present in the 1970s, with two significant changes: a greater emphasis on the democratisation of the government of Scotland and a much higher profile of the question of Scottish representation at the EU level. Democratisation remained the primary reason why the STUC advocated the establishment of a Scottish Parliament in the 1990s. Such need for democratisation was seen as having been increasingly exacerbated by the divergent electoral patterns between Scotland and England which determined the repeated election of UK Conservative governments that only commanded small minority support in Scotland. On that ground, the STUC argued that a devolved Parliament would not constitute an additional layer of government and bureaucracy but the democratisation of the Scottish Office machinery which was already in place.[17] This democratic desire only reinforced the deeper and long-standing reason for wanting Scottish government, namely Scotland's distinctiveness and the different sensitivities and preferences that stemmed from it, in Campbell Christie's words, applying 'Scottish solutions to Scottish problems'.[18]

As in the 1970s, two major areas of public policy which the STUC wanted to democratise were economic policy in general and regional policy in particular, on the basis of its long-held belief in governmental intervention in the economy.[19] It should come as no surprise that one of the key elements of the STUC's conception of how devolution could democratise economic policy was to fully involve the trades unions in the formulation of the policy.[20] To counter the widespread impression that there existed a conflict between democratic accountability and policy efficiency, the STUC argued that these were two sides of the same coin as locally decided policies would be more effective in tackling local problems.[21]

With regard to independence the STUC was still opposed to it on the ground that self-government within the UK was a more advantageous option for Scotland in both political and economic terms. However, the deeply hostile language used against it in the 1970s had gone, the 1990s discourse was more one of 'degrees' and 'nuances'. As Campbell Christie put it, 'we thought we could find Scottish solutions to Scottish problems within the context of being part of the UK . . . we didn't think we could find Scottish solutions in defence, in foreign affairs and so on'.[22] Importantly, the STUC abandoned the view that independence would be an extremely costly move for Scotland and for its working class in particular. In Christie's own words, 'independence would not be disastrous . . . the issue is more now one of . . . we don't really want to break these ties in areas where we're perfectly content with what's going on'.[23]

Perception and strategic use of the EU

Although some of its concerns were still present, the STUC's fundamental perception of the EU underwent a radical change from 'outright hostility' to 'cautious enthusiasm'[24] – and support for further integration, especially in the 'social' sphere. This change was not confined to the leadership but reached deep into the organisation and was widely shared by the grassroots activists.[25] At the time of the negotiation and ratification of the Maastricht treaty, the STUC was still concerned that the process of integration was biased towards business interests,[26] that the provisions for an independent European Central Bank were fundamentally undemocratic[27] and that Scotland was at a disadvantage within the single market.[28] The fundamental change was that by the 1990s, these aspects were seen as problems to be resolved within a broadly positive perception of the EU as opposed to being reasons for advocating withdrawal: as expressed in a resolution of the 1993 Congress: 'this Congress believes that the UK's future lies in Europe'.[29] The STUC's strong support for increased powers for the European Parliament is emblematic of this seachange.[30] Towards the second half of the 1990s, its positive perception of the EU was further reinforced. Evidence that Scotland had greatly benefited from the inflow of inward investments and the EU's continuing commitment to regional and social policies played a key role.[31] As Campbell Christie put it: 'the trade unions looked to Europe as being a means by which we could see social advance'.[32]

Equally dramatic was the changed perception of the European dimension in relation to Scottish self-government. In this second period the STUC saw the EU as clearly providing opportunities and incentives for self-government and it strategically exploited them to strengthen its case for devolution. In did so in four main ways. At the most general level, first, the STUC exploited the fact that the EU was increasingly seen as a developing multi-level political system to place the issue of a Scottish regional government firmly in the framework of European integration, thus opening a European dimension to the politics of self-government.[33] Not surprisingly, economic issues were perceived as central to the new dynamics.[34] Indeed, a survey conducted by Graham and McGrath in 1990 found 71 per cent of respondents feeling that 'Europe was the single most important issue for British trade unions'.[35] One aspect of this strategy was the commitment to 'examine ways of continuing to popularise it [its scheme for a Scottish Parliament], and to inject it into European political debate'.[36] Such 'injection' was carried out by the STUC, especially in the early 1990s, in a variety of fairly creative ways in which the EU principle of subsidiarity – see below – figured prominently. These included sending delegations to Brussels to meet the heads of the EU institutions and of the European party confederations, lobbying the London embassies of a number of EU states and staging a mass 'Scotland Demands Democracy' rally in Edinburgh on 12 December 1992 to coincide with the European Council concluding the British presidency in the second half of that year.[37]

The second aspect of this strategy was the exploitation of several features of European integration to underpin the legitimacy of the demand for self-government in Scotland with the aim of making the latter appear 'progressive' and 'European'. In that context, the principle of subsidiarity figured prominently. Not only did the STUC express strong support for subsidiarity on the ground that 'decisions which affect people's lives should be taken with their active involvement and as close to them as possible'[38] but it also argued that its adoption should lead to devolution of power from the state to the regions and local authorities: 'the subsidiarity principle should be strengthened with greater decentralisation from Brussels and national centres to regional and local centres'.[39] More specifically, the STUC seized the opportunity offered by the debate on subsidiarity to claim that the latter's implementation required the devolution of power to Scotland.[40] Furthermore, the STUC explicitly placed its discourse on subsidiarity within a 'Europe of the Regions' scenario, in which the Committee of the Regions would have a key political role.[41]

Finally, the STUC also pointed out that the process of European integration had made the experience of other European states much more relevant for the UK. These experiences showed the crucial role of regional governments and the STUC used them to argue that the Scottish demands were part of a wider European trend. Scottish self-government far from being a backward-looking, parochial goal was thus a progressive, outward-looking one.[42] These features of the European Union and of the process of integration were thus offering an opportunity to add 'European legitimacy' to the demand for self-government in Scotland and the STUC did not miss the chance to exploit them to that end.[43]

If the EU aspects discussed above can be conceptualised as opportunities to strengthen the normative case for devolution, the STUC also saw other aspects of European integration as providing material incentives to acquire self-government. Two in particular were significantly exploited. First, the STUC argued that the nature of economic competition within the single market and the constraints placed on state intervention in the economy generated the need for governmental capabilities at the regional level to foster economic competitiveness, especially in peripheral regions such as Scotland.[44] The STUC explicitly mentioned the use of governmental capabilities in relation to the management of the structural funds by claiming that 'qualitative application of the [EU] regional funds under the guidance of a Scottish Parliament and local government will, therefore, be crucial'.[45] Under the constitutional status quo and with a UK Conservative government opposed to trades union involvement, the STUC was excluded from management of the structural funds in Scotland.[46] In that context, establishing a Scottish government was seen as the only way for the STUC to regain influence on economic policies.

Secondly, the STUC argued that the increasingly wider and deeper range of EU policy competences exacerbated the need for Scotland to be represented at the Union level both effectively and democratically. The rationale for this claim was, as put by James Mitchell, political scientist at the University of Strathclyde, in a report incorporated into the programme for the 1995 Congress, as follows: 'If Scotland's interests are sufficiently different to require a Parliament then a direct Scottish input into European politics is also necessary'.[47] On this basis, not only did the STUC demand the setting up of a permanent office in Brussels to 'promote Scotland and its industries and to act as an information source'[48] but it also made clear that 'direct representation within the EC' was one of the 'powers which a Scottish Parliament must have'.[49] The 'narrow lines' of the Scotland Europa office were criticised because it did not have democratic accountability and, notably, trades union involvement.[50] The STUC also explicitly linked the issue of representation at the EU level with that of Scotland's position within the single market and the constraints placed on government intervention in the economy.[51] According to Campbell Christie, the key issue in the debate on Scotland's representation in Europe was democratic accountability rather than simply effectiveness and that was the difference between representation through a Scottish Parliament as opposed to representation through the Scottish Office controlled by the UK government.[52]

The STUC thus perceived European integration as having added a substantial European dimension to Scotland's already existing 'democratic deficit' within the UK – by shifting policy-making to the European level where Scotland was poorly represented – and therefore to have further strengthened the case for a Scottish government. In Christie's own words, 'if you keep the Westminster link then the EU dimension makes power even more distant for Scotland but if Scotland goes directly to Brussels for the issues that most affect Scottish citizens then the development of European integration can actually flatten the process of government'.[53]

The Constitutional Convention

The Constitutional Convention was the key societal player in the politics of self-government in the 1990s. The Convention brought together elected and non-elected representatives of Labour, Liberal Democrats and minor parties, representatives of local authorities and a broad range of interest groups in an umbrella organisation which was meant to be representative of the whole spectrum of Scottish society. Though the Conservatives, the SNP and most business organisations refused to join the Convention, the latter's chairman could claim that it was 'much more representative of Scotland than the Westminster Parliament is of the United Kingdom'.[54] The churches, seen as valuable non-partisan actors, were particularly influential: Norman Shanks – the convenor of the Church of Scotland's Church and Nation committee – sat on the executive committee and Canon Kenyon Wright – the head of the Episcopalian Church – became the chairman of the executive committee and a key shaper of the Convention's work. The Convention set itself the objective to produce a blueprint for a devolved Scottish assembly/Parliament on which a wide consensus within Scottish civil society was deemed to exist.[55] It started working in 1989 and produced three key documents on self-government: *A Claim of Right for Scotland* in 1988, *Towards Scotland's Parliament* in 1990 and *Scotland's Parliament, Scotland's Right* in 1995.

Self-government policy

Through these documents the Convention justified Scotland's demands for self-government and elaborated proposals for a devolved Scottish Parliament which the Labour party committed itself to implement once in office. The first document – the *Claim of Right* – declared that the Scottish people had the sovereign right to choose how Scotland was governed, hence their preferred status of the Scottish political system. The two reports of 1990 and 1995 proposed a devolved Parliament and executive taking over the responsibility for those policy areas hitherto delegated to the Scottish Office, on similar lines to the Scotland Act 1978. However, there were three significant differences between the 1979 scheme and the Convention's proposals: the new Parliament would have limited tax-varying powers, be committed to equal gender representation and, notably, be elected by a system of proportional representation.

Two other aspects set the Convention's reports apart from the devolution proposals advanced in the 1970s. The first was the antagonistic attitude and the sharply critical discourse displayed towards the UK political system. The entire work of the Convention was built on the principle of the sovereignty of the Scottish people rather than of the British constitution, the latter was routinely called – somewhat derogatorily – the English constitution and the UK was referred to as a 'secretive, centralised, self-serving super-state'.[56] The second one was the open acknowledgment that the demand for self-government could ultimately lead to Scotland's secession. The 1990 report explicitly stated that independence was a feasible option whose only problem was that not enough people supported it: 'Although the *Claim of Right* clearly acknowledges the right of the people of Scotland to opt for a wholly independent state, the Convention believes that this does not have majority support'.[57] The Convention's chairman Kenyon Wright implicitly made a similar point in discussing Scotland's position in the world: 'A Scottish Parliament, whether within or without the [British] Union would contribute much more creatively to Europe and to international affairs'.[58] This attitude of openness towards independence was also reflected in the Convention's warm relations with the SNP. Despite the latter's refusal to join, the Convention made repeated attempts to take the party on board.[59] Indeed, the spirit of consensus that prevailed within the Convention had to a large extent been made possible by the vanishing of the fear of independence, which had deeply divided the pro-self-government side in the 1970s.

In sum, the Convention's work amounted to a formalisation of the devolution option by consolidating the different schemes supported by Labour, the Liberal Democrats and various interest groups with the objective of strengthening the constitutional middle-ground vis-à-vis the more extreme options of independence and the status quo. By presenting a unitary approach and wide backing the Convention was also able to make devolution appear as a 'national' rather than as a partisan project, though the Convention did not really succeed in generating interest in its work beyond the elites.[60]

Perception and strategic use of the EU

In its reports, the Constitutional Convention portrayed the European Union as a multi-level political and economic system in which the regional level occupied an important position and placed the proposed Scottish Parliament firmly in a European context rather than in a purely British one. In its 1990 document, it recognised 'the rapid pace of change as the European Community moves towards closer economic and political union'[61] and declared: 'The Act which establishes Scotland's Parliament will define the Parliament's powers, its responsibilities, and its relationship with other decision-making bodies; principally, Westminster, the European Union and Scottish local authorities'.[62] The same perception was extended to the economic sphere: 'Scottish businesses will continue to operate within the British and European single markets'.[63]

The Convention also used the European context to underpin the case for Scottish self-government in a very similar way to the STUC. Three main linkages were emphasised. First, the Convention used the process of European integration and the experiences of other European states to strengthen the legitimacy of its demand for devolution and to attack the status quo and independence as outdated concepts. The 1990 report pointed out that both centralisation and secession were out of line with the European trend and the process of integration while devolution was fully in line with them: 'Developments within other member states towards decentralised decision-making to regional and provincial Governments are seen as parallel moves to the Convention's own proposals' while it would be against the tide of history to 're-establish a nation state at the very time Europe is moving away from this narrow concept'.[64] The principle of subsidiarity was used to the same end and figured prominently in the 1995 report: 'the Act will embody the principle of subsidiarity which, as stated in the preamble to the Maastricht Treaty on European Union, requires that decisions be taken as closely as possible to the citizens affected by those decisions'.[65] As Kenyon Wright put it to the author, by exploiting these aspects of the European dimension the Convention was 'able strongly to argue that far from being out on a limb, far from being an exception, this [regional government] was now the European way, the European trend'.[66]

Second, the existence of regional governments in several other European states was also used by the Convention to strengthen the case for self-government on economic grounds, particularly for a peripheral region such as Scotland. The Convention endorsed the widespread fears about Scotland's economic position within the EU, 'the fear that Scotland may be stranded on the edge of Europe, far from the market place, is real and urgent'.[67] It claimed that this made regional government ever more necessary if Scotland was to effectively counteract the disadvantage brought by its peripheral location as other European regions were already doing: 'in comparable circumstances in other areas of Europe with home rule Parliaments or Assemblies this proximity [between regional governments and economic actors] has proved of major economic benefit, allowing a broader and deeper mutual understanding of business and political conditions'.[68] A briefing note of the Campaign for a Scottish Parliament – a parallel organisation to, but distinct from, the Convention – put the question in even starker terms: 'in essence, a Scottish Parliament is not a desirable extra, it is absolutely essential if Scotland is to thrive in Europe. As more regions and nations such as Catalonia, Flanders and the Basque Country gain a democratic voice, Scotland must not be left behind . . . Until Scotland itself has such a voice, she will always be in the slow lane of Europe'.[69]

Third and lastly, the Convention claimed that the process of European integration had raised the importance of the representation of Scottish interests at the EU level and thus added a strong additional reason to demand a devolved Parliament. The Convention's 1990 report explicitly stated that 'an effective Scottish voice in the EEC is a pressing priority' and that an office in Brussels would not be enough. 'Scotland must also have representation through the Scottish Parliament on United Kingdom Ministerial delegations to the Council of Ministers'.[70] The report also used the issue of representation in Europe to strengthen its claim that devolution was more advantageous for Scotland than independence as it would have maximised representation by combining a direct channel through a Scottish Parliament and an indirect channel through the UK government, one of the major players in the EU: 'Scotland, using the strength of the United Kingdom and her new independence of action, would be well placed to play a full part'.[71]

In sum, the Convention perceived the EU as offering both opportunities and incentives for demanding devolved self-government as distinct from independent self-government and as opposed to the status quo and utilised several features of the European dimension to strengthen both the 'moral' and the 'utilitarian' case for devolution, broadly in line with the strategies of the other interest groups analysed above.

The business organisations

In contrast with the earlier period, in the 1990s the business organisations did not set up an umbrella group – along the lines of Scotland Is British – to coordinate their positions on self-government and mobilise public opinion. Consequently, in this section I deal with the individual organisations, drawing primarily on interviews conducted with the leaders of the Scottish Confederation of British Industry (SCBI), the Scottish Institute of Directors (SIoD), the Scottish Chambers of Commerce (SCoC), the Scottish Financial Enterprise (SFE) and the Scottish Federation of Small Businesses (SFSB).

Self-government policy

Taken as a whole, Scottish business was still opposed to self-government – both devolution and independence – in the 1990s, though there was some variation between the different organisations. This stance led the business organisations, with the exception of what is now the Federation of Small Businesses, to decline taking part in the Constitutional Convention.[72] However, in sharp contrast with 1974–79 when business was at the forefront of the No campaign, in this second period the business sector decided not to actively campaign against devolution and to take a low profile during the 1997 referendum campaign. The notable exception was Sir Bruce Pattullo's, the chairman of the Bank of Scotland, intervention against tax-varying powers.[73] According to Tom Sunter, head of the SIoD, 'business didn't feel strongly on the subject . . . across the board business was against, but there was no concerted business opposition'.[74] An important consequence of the business organisations' decision not to mobilise against devolution was that the No campaign was underfunded vis-à-vis the Yes campaign, a reversal of the 1979 situation.[75]

Though the business stance on self-government appears superficially identical to the one adopted in the 1970s, there were two main differences. First, by the 1990s the central concern of the business community was the tax-varying powers of the proposed Parliament rather than a general distaste for extra bureaucracy and over-government. Secondly, and most importantly, the strong emphasis on devolution leading to independence and the deep hostility towards the latter were no longer there. The extent of business opposition to devolution clearly emerges from two surveys conducted by the Edinburgh Chamber of Commerce and the Scottish Chambers of Commerce, respectively, in 1992 and 1997. The first one found that only 15 per cent of its members considered devolution to be the best constitutional option for business while 14 per cent thought independence was best and a full 70 per cent supported the status quo.[76] Broadly similar figures emerged from the 1997 survey which found only 14 per cent of respondents thinking that devolution – with or without tax-varying powers – would have improved business policy and the business environment in Scotland, against 45 per cent and 76 per cent thinking the opposite, for devolution without tax-varying powers and with tax-varying powers, respectively.[77] Qualitative evidence emerging from my interviews and findings of previous studies point in the same direction.[78] Business opposition to self-government was still to a large extent caused by traditional scepticism about benefits to be derived from multi-layered government – as the director of the Scottish Chambers of Commerce put it: 'businesses generally do not like overgovernment, they do not want a lot of layers of government'[79] – but what had become the focus of their concerns was the prospect of differential taxation between Scotland and England which would have put Scotland-based businesses at a competitive disadvantage.[80]

The business organisations were still opposed to secession, which they regarded as a costly and disruptive move for the business sector itself but also for the Scottish economy as a whole. However, as mentioned above, the intensity of this opposition was much weaker than in 1979. At that time it was the key determinant of their stance on devolution while by the 1990s it was a secondary issue. Qualitative evidence of this 'softening' of attitudes is provided by the fact that the linkage between devolution and independence was replaced by the taxation issue as the central plank of the business discourse against devolution. Indeed, in so far as business leaders spoke up against devolution, they specifically targeted the tax-varying powers rather than the principle of devolution itself. Additional, quantitative evidence is contained in the results of the 1997 survey mentioned above, which show that the degree of opposition to self-government changed much more between devolution without tax-varying powers and devolution with tax-varying powers than between the latter and independence. Indeed, 15.5 per cent thought independence would have improved the business environment against 13.5 per cent who thought the same of devolution with tax-varying powers.

If these elements were broadly common to all business organisations, there were also some differences between them. Two main divides can be identified. The first was between the organisations representing large and small companies with the Scottish CBI, the Scottish IoD and the SFE on one side and the Chambers of Commerce and, especially, the SFSB on the other side. Large companies were more hostile than small companies to self-government. This was reflected in the fact that the SFSB, as seen above, was the only business organisation which joined the Constitutional Convention and also in the positions taken during the referendum campaign.[81] It appears that this was so as a result of two characteristics which set small and large companies apart: the degree of rootedness in the territory and the perceived distance from government. Small companies were overwhelmingly Scottish both in terms of operations and of market while large companies were British companies which just happened to be based in Scotland.[82] Likewise, small companies felt they had very difficult access to government under the constitutional status quo and welcomed devolution as a way of bringing government closer to them while large companies had the resources to access the UK government so did not feel the advantages of closer government to the same extent.[83] The second divide was between industrial and financial companies, the latter represented by the SFE. Financial companies were the most hostile towards self-government largely because they perceived any constitutional change to be detrimental to their business which was both very sensitive, especially life assurance, and very highly geared towards the English market.[84] Financial services companies also did not see any advantage from having devolved government as the key governmental decisions that affect their business were among the reserved competences of the UK government, and they were uninterested in the European dimension on the ground that no single European market existed for financial products.[85]

The business organisations' decision to adopt a low profile and not actively campaign against devolution was determined by a significant change of attitudes towards independence. Independence came to be seen as an option little different from devolution with tax-varying powers, at least as far as the business sector was concerned, and no longer as an economic disaster for Scotland.

Perception and strategic use of the EU

The Scottish business sector still had an overall positive perception of the European Union in the 1990s. However, this overall perception masked two very different elements: attitudes towards economic integration and attitudes towards political integration, especially as regards its social dimension. On the one hand, not surprisingly, attitudes to economic integration were still very positive, with broad agreement that Scotland had benefited from the development of the single internal market, which had facilitated trade with mainland Europe and had attracted a substantial inflow of foreign direct investment into Scotland. On the other hand, there were widespread concerns about the burden that single-market regulations, particularly those relating to social policy, were putting on Scottish companies. It appears that business attitudes towards the EU in the 1990s were essentially dictated by their traditional support for free trade and their traditional opposition to government regulation of the economy. As the EU developed the second aspect of integration to a significant extent in the 1990s, perceptions of European integration became dichotomous.

The business organisations perceived only tenuous links to exist between the European Union and the question of Scotland's constitutional status hence the European dimension did not influence their position to any significant extent, at least directly. Companies no longer perceived Scottish self-government as being antithetical to the process of European integration nor did they still perceive the European dimension as placing practical constraints on devolution, apart from the rather obvious point that higher taxes would have put Scottish companies at a disadvantage vis-à-vis their English and their European rivals. On the other hand, they did not see the European dimension as offering any opportunity or incentive for regional government either, though some of them – particularly small companies – acknowledged the advantage of a more effective representation of Scottish interests at the Union level.

There were thus two crucial differences from the strategy they adopted in the 1970s. First, they could no longer use the European dimension against devolution by claiming that this was an outdated and parochial move for the dominant understanding was by then that regional government was very much part of the European trend, as embodied in the 'Europe of the Regions' concept. Second, they could no longer exploit the fear of secession to undermine support for devolution as the former, now firmly placed in the European context, lost almost all of the negative connotations it had had in the 1970s. Indeed, there is evidence that this perception was widespread within the business sector itself and may explain their decision not to fight the No corner in the 1997 referendum. The fact that independence was perceived in no more negative terms than devolution with tax-varying powers in the 1990s is highly likely to be due to the fact that independence was by then placed in a radically different political and economic context.

Conclusions

The interest groups supporting devolution – the Church of Scotland and the STUC – had a much greater influence on the politics of self-government in 1988–97 than those opposing it – the business organisations. This was because the former played a leading role in the Constitutional Convention and were thus able to use the Convention as a 'multiplier' of their ability to influence both the political parties and, to a lesser extent, public opinion. The Convention strengthened interest groups' influence on political parties as interest group' participation and agreement was crucial to substantiate claims that the Convention was representative of – and thus entitled to speak on behalf of – Scottish civil society as a whole not just of its political class. This gave interest groups a leverage vis-à-vis political parties that they did not have in the 1970s.[86] In contrast, the business organisations – which had been key players in the 1970s – remained largely on the sidelines and did not even forge an effective partnership with the Conservative party with the result that the latter, as seen in the previous chapter, fought the No campaign virtually in isolation.

The European dimension figured much more prominently than in the 1970s in the interest groups' strategies and, furthermore, it played the positive role of underpinning the demand for self-government. This was because a key player in the pro-self-government front – the STUC – was by then perceiving the European dimension as providing both opportunities and incentives for Scottish self-government and decided to exploit them in its strategy. The new position thus put the STUC alongside the Church of Scotland in seeing the European Union as a facilitator of regional self-government and this, enhanced by the same position adopted by the Constitutional Convention, resulted in the European dimension figuring prominently in the pro-self-government discourse.

The new 'framing' of the connection between European integration and Scottish self-government produced by the changed attitudes towards the European Union and, especially, by the perception that supra-state integration and sub-state devolution of power were 'two sides of the same coin', allowed the pro-self-government camp to gain a strategic advantage. The Yes side was thus able to exploit many aspects of the process of integration to strengthen the case for self-government while preventing their opponents from using Europe to attack devolution, as happened in the 1970s.

Notes

1 Shanks (1996: 19).
2 Shanks, interview with the author.
3 Church of Scotland (1989: 144).
4 Ibidem: 145.
5 Shanks (1996: 31).
6 Church of Scotland (1989: 170–1).
7 See in particular ibidem: 171–3.
8 Church of Scotland (1996: 11, 33).
9 Church of Scotland (1989: 149, and also 1989: 151, 1993: 21, 1997: 17).
10 Church of Scotland (1989: 172).
11 Herron (1989: 28).
12 See Aitken (1997: 309, and 292–304).
13 Quoted in Aitken (1997: 283; see also 302 and 309).
14 STUC (1997: 36).
15 See STUC (1993: 161; also 1995: 175).
16 See, for example, STUC (1993: 161–3).
17 STUC (1992: 72; also 1995: 175).
18 Christie, interview with the author.
19 STUC (1992: 51, 67, 1993: 71–2).
20 STUC (1992: 51, 1995: 73).
21 Ibidem both references as note 20.
22 Christie, interview with the author.
23 Ibidem; see also Aitken (1997: 306).
24 Graham and McGrath (1991: 61).
25 Ibidem: 66.
26 STUC (1992: 66; also 1995: 177).
27 STUC (1993: 74).
28 STUC (1992: 67, 1993: 71–3); see also Graham and McGrath (1991: 67).
29 STUC (1994: 170); see also Graham and McGrath (1991: 60).
30 STUC (1995: 177).
31 See STUC (1992: 95, 1993: 74, 92, 1994: 170, 1995: 73, 1997: 22); see also Graham and McGrath (1991: 65).
32 Christie, interview with the author.
33 STUC (1993: 161, 1996: 3).

34 *The Trades Union Agenda for a Scottish Parliament – Scotland's Economic Development*, p. 2. See also Graham and McGrath (1991: 59).
35 Graham and McGrath (1991: 65).
36 STUC (1993: 161, 1994: 163).
37 See STUC (1993: 162–3 and 1994: 164).
38 STUC (1992: 72).
39 STUC (1993: 74).
40 See STUC (1993: 74, 1994: 163).
41 STUC (1993: 74).
42 Christie, interview with the author.
43 Ibidem.
44 STUC (1992: 67).
45 Ibidem.
46 See STUC (1995: 74; also 1997: 22–3). Moreover, the STUC was unable to negotiate union recognition with inward investors through the Locate in Scotland agency, see Aitken (1997: 285).
47 STUC *Congress Programme* (1995: 10).
48 STUC (1992: 51).
49 *A Power for Change* (1991: 8); see also STUC (1993: 74).
50 On Scotland Europa see Mitchell (1995).
51 *A Power for Change* (1991: 11–12).
52 Christie, interview with the author.
53 Ibidem.
54 Wright (1997: 53).
55 For an insider account of the Convention's work, see Wright (1997); for academic analyses see, among others, Kellas (1992).
56 *Scotland's Parliament, Scotland's Right*, p. 31.
57 *Towards Scotland's Parliament*, p. 7.
58 Wright (1989: 35).
59 On the attitude towards the SNP, see Shanks (1996: 29).
60 See also Kellas (1992: 53–4).
61 *Towards Scotland's Parliament*, p. 8.
62 *Scotland's Parliament, Scotland's Right*, p. 12.
63 Ibidem, p. 29.
64 *Towards Scotland's Parliament*, p. 8.
65 *Scotland's Parliament, Scotland's Right*, p. 12.
66 Wright, interview with the author.
67 *Towards Scotland's Parliament*, pp. 8–9.
68 *Scotland's Parliament, Scotland's Right*, p. 29.
69 Campaign for a Scottish Parliament, briefing note no. 7, National Library of Scotland, Acc. 11497.
70 *Towards Scotland's Parliament*, p. 8; see also *Scotland's Parliament, Scotland's Right*, p. 16.
71 *Towards Scotland's Parliament*, p. 8.
72 See Lynch (1998: 89).
73 See Dardanelli (2002: 202).
74 Sunter, interview with the author.
75 See, among others, Mitchell et al. (1998: 175).

76 Edinburgh Chamber of Commerce (1992: 6).
77 Scottish Chambers of Commerce (1997: 5); for additional data, see Lynch (1998).
78 Interviews with Allan Hogarth, SCBI; Lex Gold, SCoC; Tom Sunter, SIoD, John Downie, FSB; Ray Perman, SFE; see also Lynch (1998).
79 Gold, interview with the author; also Sunter, Hogarth and Perman, interviews with the author.
80 Ibidem, references as note 79.
81 On the latter point, see for example ' "Who Pays New Tax?" asks CBI chief ', *The Scotsman*, 8 September 1997.
82 Downie and Sunter, interviews with the author.
83 Downie, interview with the author.
84 Perman, interview with the author.
85 Ibidem.
86 On this point, see also Paterson et al. (1992: 633).

8
Public opinion

Like in the 1970s, in this latter period too, public opinion closely matched elite opinion though more as regards perceptions of the European Union than in relation to self-government. The sharp turnaround in attitudes towards the EU seen in the case of Labour, the STUC and the SNP and the emergence of a split among the Conservatives was almost exactly mirrored at the mass public level as shown by segmentation by party identification. In contrast, the distribution of constitutional preferences was less closely linked to party identification, in particular as regards independence whose popularity reached well beyond the group of Nationalist identifiers. Indeed, the relative decline of devolution and the sharp rise of independence were the two key changes between the 1970s and the 1990s. Coupled with the change in attitudes towards the EU, these variations led to a far-reaching re-shaping of public opinion. By the 1990s, support for self-government was associated with support for the EU, independence – 'in Europe' – was the second most popular constitutional option and, crucially, was preferred to the status quo as second best. Despite the fact that devolution was still perceived to be likely to lead to independence, this re-shaping of mass preferences neutralised the 'interaction effect' and led to a strong endorsement of devolution in the 1997 referendum. For the sake of comparison with the earlier period, in the analysis below I use as much as possible the same variables employed in chapter 4.

The demand for self-government

Voters considered self-government to be not very important in 1997. Indeed, its perceived importance was lower than in 1979, across all party identifications. There also was little variation between those identifying with the UK-wide parties, with a majority – or close to a majority – of Conservative, Liberal and Labour identifiers thinking it was not very important or not at all important.

Table 8.1 Importance of self-government by party identification (column %), 1997

Q. When you were deciding about voting in the general election, how important was this issue – Scottish Parliament – to you? Was it . . .

Importance	Conservative	Labour	Liberal	Nationalist	All
Not important*	62	47	56	16	46
Important	26	36	34	39	33
Extremely important	8	15	8	41	16
Don't know	4	2	2	4	4
N	140	397	90	140	882

Note: *For ease of comparability with 1979, it also includes the category 'not at all important'.
Source: Scottish Election Survey 1997.

As in 1979, Nationalist identifiers were an outlier group, with the modal category being 'extremely important' and only 16 per cent judging it unimportant (table 8.1).

In contrast, support for self-government was very widely based, significantly more so than in 1979. Aggregate support for all self-government options stood at 78 per cent, with the two preferred options being a devolved Parliament with tax-varying powers and independence in Europe with 34 and 26 per cent support, respectively. Compared to 1979, these data indicate a decline in support for devolution – from 54 to 43 per cent – and a five-fold jump in support for independence, from 7 to 35 per cent. As in 1979, there was significant variation by party identification. Conservative identifiers expressed a very clear opposition to self-government with over 60 per cent preference for the status quo and very limited support for both devolution and independence. Among the 'devolutionists', the small group of Liberal identifiers had a majority preference for devolution but the lowest support for independence of all and a sizeable support for the status quo while the large group of Labour identifiers also had majority support for devolution – with clear preference for the tax-varying option – but it also expressed a substantial 36 per cent support for independence. Lastly, Nationalist identifiers were virtually unanimous in supporting self-government with majority preference for independence in the EU followed by around 20 per cent support for both devolution with tax-varying powers and independence outside the EU (table 8.2).

In even sharper contrast to 1979, however, the referendum vote closely mirrored the pattern of support for self-government. Over 50 per cent of the electorate voted Yes against only 18 per cent voting No while

Table 8.2 Support for self-government by party identification (column %), 1997

Q. Which of these statements* comes closest to your view . . . Scotland should?

Statement	Conservative	Labour	Liberal	Nationalist	All
Status quo	61	7	35	2	19
Devolution	27	53	53	25	43
Parliament no tax	11	8	18	5	9
Parliament with tax	16	45	35	20	34
Independence	9	36	8	72	35
Independence in EU	8	26	8	54	26
Independence out EU	1	10	0	18	9
Self-government	36	89	61	89	78
Don't know	2	4	4	9	3
N	123	336	51	122	676

Note: *Scotland should remain part of the UK without an elected Parliament; Scotland should remain part of the UK, with its own elected Parliament which has no taxation powers; Scotland should remain part of the UK, with its own elected Parliament which has some taxation powers; Scotland should become independent, separate from the UK but part of the European Union; Scotland should become independent, separate from the UK and the European Union.
Source: Scottish and Welsh Referendum Studies 1997.

26 per cent did not vote. The voting pattern by party identification shows very large majorities in favour of devolution among Labour and, especially, Nationalist identifiers and a clear majority against among the Conservatives. The small group of Liberal identifiers, somewhat surprisingly, displayed a more balanced pattern, with 47 per cent voting Yes and 31 per cent voting No (table 8.3).

No 'interaction effect' turning support for self-government into rejection of devolution was thus at play in 1997, as only very small numbers of supporters of self-government voted No in the referendum. Two further elements stand in sharp contrast to 1979: the balance between support for devolution and support for independence and the pattern of voting of the two groups. Among supporters of self-government, 55 per cent favoured devolution while 45 per cent were in favour of independence – the corresponding figures were 89 and 11 per cent, respectively, in 1979. This further illustrates that independence was dramatically more popular than eighteen years before, as mentioned above. Moreover, the voting patterns of the two groups had become virtually identical, with only marginally more devolutionists voting No in the referendum, as opposed to the mass rejection witnessed in 1979 (table 8.4).

Table 8.3 Referendum vote by party identification (column %), 1997

Q. How did you vote on the first question*?

Vote	Conservative	Labour	Liberal	Nationalist	All
Voted No	**58**	7	31	1	**18**
Didn't vote	25	26	22	20	26
Voted Yes	**15**	66	47	78	**55**
Don't know/					
no answer	2	1	0	1	1
N	123	336	51	122	676

Note: *Should there be a Scottish Parliament in the UK?
Source: Scottish and Welsh Referendum Studies 1997.

Table 8.4 Referendum vote of supporters of self-government (column %), 1997

Q. How did you vote on the first question*?

Vote	Devolution	Independence	All
Voted Yes	65	75	70
Didn't vote	28	23	25
Voted No	7	2	5
N	289	232	521

Note: *Should there be a Scottish Parliament in the UK?
Source: Scottish and Welsh Referendum Studies 1997.

This was despite the fact that voters still seemed to think that devolution was likely to facilitate the 'slide' towards independence. Questioned on what the new Parliament should not bring about, voters overwhelmingly cited making leaving the UK more likely as the key issue. Further analysis shows that this was even more acutely felt among opponents of devolution (table 8.5).

The crucial difference appears to be that in 1997 the second preference of devolutionists was independence instead of the status quo – while the opposite was the case in 1979. As the data indicate, Nationalist identifiers, not surprisingly, were unanimous in their preference for independence while among both Labour and Liberal identifiers those preferring independence as second best outnumbered those preferring the status quo by more than two to one. Conservative identifiers were an outlier group in preferring the status quo but even among them a non-negligible 15 per cent would have settled for independence (table 8.6).[1]

Table 8.5 Parliament's most important thing not to do by vote in the referendum (column %), 1997

Q. This card shows a few things a Scottish Parliament might want to bring about . . . And which, if any, should a Scottish Parliament *not* try to bring about? IF SEVERAL MENTIONED: Which is the most important?

	Yes	*No*	*All*
Leave UK more likely	47	85	56
Stronger voice in UK	3	1	2
Stronger voice in EU	1	1	1
More pride in country	1	2	1
Increase standard of living	1	0	1
None of these	32	5	25
Others/Don't know	15	6	14

Note: N = 676.
Source: Scottish and Welsh Referendum Studies 1997.

Table 8.6 Second preference of supporters of devolution by party identification (column %), 1997

Q. And which would be your second preference?

Preference	*Conservative*	*Labour*	*Liberal*	*Nationalist*	*All*
Independence	**15**	**31**	**40**	**33**	**30**
Independence outside EU	0	6	8	4	5
Independence within EU	15	25	32	29	25
Other devolution option*	46	32	24	50	34
Status quo	**27**	**16**	**12**	**0**	**17**
Don't know/no answer	12	21	24	17	20
N	33	168	25	24	289

Note: *with tax-varying powers and vice versa.
Source: Scottish and Welsh Referendum Studies 1997.

Attitudes towards the UK and the EU

As for 1979, in this section I use satisfaction with government, perception of Scotland's welfare and identification with the UK to estimate Scots' attitudes towards the UK political system in its political, economic and symbolic dimensions. As regards attitudes to the EU, three measures are available for 1997: satisfaction with membership, support for the 'social dimension' as proxied by support for the Social Chapter and identification with Europe. Satisfaction with membership is largely a measure of support for economic integration, i.e. for the establishment of an integrated single market.[2] Support for the Social Chapter, on the other hand, is a key indicator of support for adding an explicitly political dimension to the EU's public policy. Like the UK variables, these variables thus also intend to measure attitudes towards the EU in its economic, political and symbolic dimensions.

Attitudes to the UK were negative in all three variables, but considerable variation existed between variables, across party identifications and relative to 1979. Satisfaction with government was only marginally negative but Scotland was still widely perceived as being less well off than the rest of the UK and voters overwhelmingly identified primarily with Scotland as opposed to with the UK as a whole. Disaggregating by party identification one finds, as expected, Conservative identifiers at one end of the spectrum, with broadly positive attitudes, and Nationalist identifiers at the other end, with solidly negative opinions. Labour and Liberal identifiers occupied the middle ground, the former closer to the Nationalists and the latter to the Conservatives. Somewhat less expectedly, Labour identifiers were much more likely to identify primarily with Scotland than Liberal ones while Liberals had a more negative opinion of the UK political system than Labour identifiers had. It thus appears that Scots had a very strong primary identification with Scotland while they had more mildly negative attitudes towards the political and economic aspects of the UK polity. In comparison to 1979, these data paint a three-fold change. First, satisfaction with the UK political system sharply deteriorated, notably so among Conservative and Liberal identifiers, though, somewhat surprisingly, it improved among Nationalists. Second, despite remaining mostly negative, the perception of Scotland's welfare vis-à-vis the rest of the UK improved a great deal across the board, especially so among Conservatives. Third, primary national identification directed itself even more clearly towards Scotland rather than towards the UK as a whole, most notably among Labour identifiers (table 8.7).

Moving on to analyse attitudes to the EU, the data indicate that respondents expressed both satisfaction with membership and support for the Social Chapter but an extremely limited degree of identification with Europe. On the first and the third variables, variation across party identification was minimal whereas sharp divisions existed with regard to the Social Chapter between Labour, Nationalists and, to a lesser extent, Liberals, on the positive side, and Conservatives on the negative side. Assuming the first variable is broadly comparable with the 1979 one, these findings suggest that Labour and Nationalists had radically changed their perception of the economic dimension of the EU and supported a 'social dimension' to it while Liberal and, especially, Conservative identifiers remained positive towards the former but rejected the latter. They also suggest that the process of integration had

Table 8.7 Attitudes to the UK by party identification (indices), 1997

Satisfaction with government:
Q. Which of these statements† best describes your opinion on the present system of governing Britain?
Perception of Scotland's welfare:
Q. Compared with other parts of Britain, would do you say that these days Scotland is better off, not so well off or just about the same?
Identification with the UK:
Q. Which, if any, of the following‡ best describes how you see yourself?

Statement	*Conservative*	*Labour*	*Liberal*	*Nationalist*	*All*
Satisfaction with govt*	41	−4	−14	−24	−1
Scotland's welfare**	3	−37	−25	−39	−28
Identification with the UK***	−21	−66	−23	−83	−58

Notes: †Works extremely well and could not be improved; Could be improved in small ways but mainly works well; Could be improved quite a lot; Needs a great deal of improvement; ‡Scottish, not British; Scottish more than British; Equally Scottish and British; British more than Scottish; British not Scottish. I collapsed the first two categories into a primary identification with Scotland and the latter into a primary identification with the UK. *Index varies between −200 = all respondents were very dissatisfied and +200 = all respondents were very satisfied, data are relative to General Election. **index varies between −100 = 100% of respondents thought Scotland was worse off than the rest of the UK and +100 = 100% of respondents thought Scotland was better off, data are relative to Referendum. ***index varies between −100 = 100% of respondents identified primarily with Scotland and +100 = 100% of respondents identified primarily with the UK, data are relative to referendum.
Sources: Scottish Election Survey 1997 and Scottish and Welsh Referendum Studies 1997.

close to no impact on collective identifications as public perceptions of the EU remained largely confined to the economic and political aspects. As regards the connections between attitudes to the EU and attitudes to the UK, these results indicate that Scots perceived the UK and the EU as broadly consistent in the economic sphere but sharply in contrast in political terms, notably as regards the social dimension (table 8.8).

Determinants of the referendum vote

To test the determinants of the Yes vote in the 1997 referendum I again use logistic regressions. As explained in chapter 4, this multi-variate statistical technique enables the researcher to test the association between a number of independent variables and a dichotomous dependent variable, such as a referendum vote. A statistically significant positive association between a given category against the 'base' category for each independent variable indi-

Table 8.8 – Attitudes to the EU by party identification (indices), 1997

Satisfaction with membership
Q. On the whole, do you think the European Union has been . . . Good for Scotland, Bad for Scotland, Neither good nor bad?
Support for the Social Chapter
Q. Which of these statements† comes closest to your view?
Identification with Europe
Q. Do you think of yourself as European?

Statement	*Conservative*	*Labour*	*Liberal*	*Nationalist*	*All*
Satisfaction with membership*	30	30	41	35	32
Support for Social Chapter**	−39	33	26	34	19
Identification with Europe***	−70	−82	−54	−78	−76

Notes: †The British government *should sign up* to the Social Chapter so that British workers have the same rights at work as everyone else in Europe; the British government *should not sign up* to the Social Chapter because it would cost too many British workers their jobs; can't choose. *Index varies between −100 = 100% of respondents thought membership of the EU had been bad for Scotland and +100 = 100% of respondents thought it had been good for Scotland, data are relative to the referendum. **Index varies between −100 = 100% of respondents thought the UK should not sign up and +100 = 100% of respondents thought the UK should sign up, data are relative to the general election. ***Index varies between −100 = 0% of respondents thought of themselves as Europeans and +100= 100% of respondents thought of themselves as Europeans, data are relative to the referendum.
Sources: Scottish Election Survey 1997 and Scottish and Welsh Referendum Studies 1997.

cates that voters possessing that characteristic were more likely than those in the 'base' category to have voted Yes rather than No in the referendum. I use broadly the same explanatory variable as for 1979, with the exception of those related to attitudes to independence – not available for 1997 – and some minor changes, as follows: government popularity is now proxied by attitudes towards the Labour party, attitudes to the UK political system are proxied by trust in the UK government to work in Scotland's interest and attitudes to the EU are measured by satisfaction with membership.

The results indicate that only three variables had a statistically significant independent effect on the Yes vote. As in 1979, partisanship was a key factor: Labour, Liberal and, especially, Nationalist identifiers were much more likely than Conservatives to have endorsed devolution. Even more powerful than in 1979, however, was the influence of attitudes towards self-government. Supporters of a Parliament with tax-varying powers and of independence, in particular, were very much more likely to have voted Yes than those in favour of the status quo. In contrast to the previous referendum, national identity also seemed to have played a role with primary Scottish identifiers more likely to have voted Yes than primary British identifiers. Attitudes to the UK and the EU do not appear to have had an independent effect and were most likely mediated by partisanship. In a similar fashion to 1979, neither the perception of Scotland's economic situation nor attitudes to the Labour party nor the sociological variables – with the exception of national identity – had a meaningful impact, either substantively or statistically. The 'cleaner' nature of the 1997 referendum also transpires from the fact that a very parsimonious three-variable model is able to correctly predict 95 per cent of the cases in the dependent variable (table 8.9).

Table 8.9 Logistic regression models of Yes voting in the 1997 referendum

Variable	Model 1	Model 2
Party identification (base: Conservative)		
Labour	2.554**	2.793***
Liberal Democrat	2.845**	2.765**
Nationalist	4.587**	4.576**
Constitutional preferences (base: status quo)		
Parliament, no tax-varying	4.977***	4.627***
Parliament, tax-varying	6.088***	5.581***
Independence in the EU	6.284***	5.884***
Independence outside the EU	6.141***	5.530***
Scotland's welfare (base: not so well off)		
As well off as the rest of the UK	0.364	
Better off than the rest of the UK	−0.108	
Attitudes to the Labour party (base: none/other/don't know)		
Favour strongly	0.425	
Favour	−0.587	
Against	−0.939	
Strongly against	−1.321	
Trust in the UK government (base: almost never)		
Some of the time	−1.606	
Most of the time	−1.035	
Just about always	−1.800	
Satisfaction with EU membership (base: neither good nor bad)		
Bad	−1.320	
Good	−0.598	
Class (base: working)		
Middle	−0.349	
None/don't know	−0.277	
National identity† (base: British)		
Scottish	1.117^	0.874^

Table 8.9 (continued)

Variable	Model 1	Model 2
Religion (base: none/other/don't know)		
Roman Catholic	1.502	
Church of Scotland	−0.15	
Constant	−3.528	−5.379
−2 log likelihood	127.591	151.588
Pseudo-r^2 (Nagelkerke)	0.839	0.816
Percentage correctly predicted	95.4	94.9

Notes: ***Significant at p < 0.001. **Significant at p < 0.01. *Significant at p < 0.05. ^Significant at p < 0.10. †For the sake of comparability with 1979, I re-grouped the original five categories into two categories as follows: British not Scottish = British; British more than Scottish = British; equally British and Scottish = British; more Scottish than British = Scottish; Scottish not British = Scottish. Interaction effects among the explanatory variables were tested for and found not significant, the results are not reported here but are available from the author.

Conclusions

The findings discussed in this chapter show that the 1997 referendum was a much more 'straightforward' affair than the 1979 one. There was strong and widespread support for self-government at the time of the referendum and this was translated into a very clear endorsement of devolution in the vote. No 'interaction effect' was generated. Despite the fact that many elements remained remarkably stable between the two points in time – notably the perception than devolution would facilitate independence – two crucial elements set the 1997 patterns of opinion and voting in contrast to the 1979 ones. First, independence was a much more popular constitutional option, attracting almost as many supporters as devolution itself. Secondly, devolutionists were no longer fearful of secession, they actually preferred it to the status quo.

The results also indicate that independence was much more popular than in 1979 because it was 'in Europe', i.e. it was placed within the positive context of an evolving European Union. In contrast to 1979, supporters of self-government identifying with Labour and the SNP had a very positive perception of the EU in general terms and of its emerging 'social dimension' in particular. In this respect, as in others, public perceptions were closely in line with attitudes and positions of elite political actors, as discussed in the previous chapters.

Lastly, the 'democratic deficit' thesis, according to which the explanation for the endorsement of devolution in the 1997 referendum relative to its rejection in the 1979 one is to be found in the 'democratic deficit' created by eighteen years of Conservative rule which was consistently rejected in Scotland, does not find empirical support. Satisfaction with government declined more sharply among Conservatives than among other groups of party identifiers and actually increased among Nationalists. Partly as a consequence, trust in the UK government was not a strong determinant of the referendum vote. Moreover, the importance of self-government as a political issue declined between the two points in time and support for devolution itself actually fell. As discussed above, it was the rise in popularity of independence, and its ramifications, which was the crucial determinant of the difference between the two referendum outcomes.

Notes

1 Given the small number of Conservative, Liberal and Nationalist identifiers, these results should be treated with caution.
2 See, among others, Gabel (1998).

9
Successful Europeanisation in the 1990s

In sharp contrast to the 1970s, the European dimension had a very significant impact on the politics of Scottish self-government in the 1990s. All elite actors, including those opposing devolution, identified important links between the two issues and tried to exploit the European dimension to their advantage, thus turning devolution into a 'three-level game'. In a reversal of the 1979 situation, this process of Europeanisation was a factor of unity and strength on the Yes side and had far-reaching consequences for the outcome of the 1997 referendum. The evidence suggests that the exploitation of the European dimension was the single most important factor accounting for the endorsement of devolution in 1997 relative to its rejection in 1979.

Elite actors

This process of Europeanisation was rooted in the fact that the key elite actors of the SNP, the Labour party and the STUC all radically changed their attitudes to the EU, from deep hostility to mild enthusiasm. This brought about consistency between support for European integration and for Scottish self-government and made 'visible' to them the many properties of the EU dimension that could be used to strengthen the case for self-government. Once the re-alignment had taken place, the pro-devolution elite actors – with the SNP at their forefront – set out to fully exploit the European dimension by adding an explicit European side to their policies. As discussed below, this had a profound and ultimately crucial impact on public opinion.

Positive perception of the EU

Pro-self-government actors had a positive perception of the European Union, in relation to four aspects in particular: economic integration, supra-state governance, the social dimension and the respective positions of the EU and UK relative to Scotland. Despite lingering concerns about peripherality, the building of a single market was perceived as having been beneficial for Europe in general and for Scotland in particular. Supra-state governance was seen as a necessary feature of a modern political order in Europe, in particular in the new post-Cold War order and vis-à-vis the process of globalisation, though, again, concerns with specific aspects such as the EMU criteria of the Maastricht treaty were still present. The EU institutions were seen as the top tier of the EU multi-level political system in which regional governments had a prominent place and state governments were no longer the only players. The emerging social dimension was welcomed as an overdue complement to the pro-business bias of integration and as a way of by-passing the policies of the Conservative government in London. Lastly, but most importantly, primarily because of its social and regional policies, the EU was then perceived to be to the left of the UK system and therefore closer to Scottish preferences than the latter. From a left-of-centre Scottish perspective – shared to a varying extent by the whole pro-self-government front – the EU came to be construed as a 'positive alternative' to the Conservative-governed UK, rather than as a 'negative extension' of it, as in the 1970s. In this light, the shortcomings of the EU such as the agricultural policy or the so-called 'democratic deficit' were by then seen as 'problems to be resolved' rather than 'reasons to leave'.

In contrast, the Conservative party and the business sector remained positive on economic integration but strongly rejected the social dimension. As the latter grew in visibility and salience, its influence in shaping how the EU was perceived also grew, leading to growing scepticism among Conservatives and business. This had three effects. First, support for the EU became increasingly associated with the demand for self-government and a split attitude – but with strong negative overtones – became associated with opposition to devolution. Secondly, it led to a radical re-assessment of the relevance of the European Union to Scottish self-government. From being perceived as a threat, the EU came to be perceived as an opportunity. More particularly, it came to be perceived as a facilitator of self-government, providing incentives and offering opportunities for both independence and devolution. Thirdly, this pattern of attitudes meant that the European dimension became an element of unity on the pro-devolution side and an element of division among their opponents, thus deepening the gap between the two sides. All three of these aspects constituted a neat reversal of the 1970s situation.

Awareness of the EU's opportunities and incentives

As a result of the new perception described above, the pro-self-government actors were by then well aware of the incentives and opportunities the EU was offering for both independence and devolution.

With regard to independence, the SNP identified four key aspects, the first three providing incentives and the fourth offering an opportunity. First, a wide range of policy-making competences that had previously been exercised at the state level was by then exercised at the Union level. Second, the key institutional actors at that level were still – if not even more so – the Council of Ministers and the European Council in which only state governments are represented. Third, the entire institutional structure of the EU was biased in favour of the small states which are over-represented in the key institutions of the Commission, Parliament, Court and Council and have a right of veto in the latter over a wide range of policy areas. Taken together, these three politico-institutional factors were providing powerful incentives to acquire statehood, the only constitutional status which would have allowed Scotland to fully benefit from the EU institutional environment. In the eyes of the SNP, they were thus providing additional reasons for demanding independence. The fourth aspect pertained to the economic sphere and was constituted by the fact that the EU provided a customs union and a single internal market. The customs union and the single market would guarantee free trade and regulatory continuity in the economic relationship between an independent Scotland and the rest of the EU, the rest of the UK in particular. This aspect was perceived by the SNP as dramatically lowering the economic costs for Scotland of seceding from the UK. It was thus offering the opportunity to acquire independence without many of the costs traditionally associated with such a move. For the SNP this was the most powerful of the facilitating aspects of the EU.

With regard to devolution, the Labour party and the other devolutionist actors identified three main aspects. The first two provided incentives and the last one offered an opportunity. First, the wide range of policy-making competences exercised at the Union level was also identified by the devolutionists as sharpening the need for adequate representation of Scottish interests at that level. On the assumption that only a devolved government which also retained access to the UK level would be in a position to do so, the pro-devolution actors perceived this aspect as providing additional reasons for demanding devolution. In other words, not only was devolution necessary to properly govern Scotland but also to properly represent it at the Union level. Second, the constraints placed by EU rules on the extent to which state governments could intervene in the economy created a keener need for governmental action

at the regional level. Again, on the assumption that only a devolved government would be able to perform this function, the devolutionists perceived this
aspect as providing an additional reason for their demands. Finally, the widespread rhetoric about the idea of a 'Europe of the Regions', with institutional
aspects linked to it such as the Committee of the Regions and the principle of
subsidiarity, and the high profile of many processes of regionalisation across
Europe, were perceived as providing ample legitimation for Scottish demands.
The establishment of the Committee of the Regions generated expectations
that regions would play a much more prominent role in EU's policy-making
while the principle of subsidiarity gave powerful normative justification to the
idea that power could and should be devolved from state governments to
regional governments. By tying the concept of regional self-government to the
process of European integration – the modernising European political project
par excellence – the idea of a 'Europe of the Regions' removed the inward-
and backward-looking label of regional government and, in stark contrast to
the 1970s, made it part of the contemporary zeitgeist. In the eyes of the pro-
devolution actors, the European dimension thus provided a welcome opportunity to add legitimacy to their demands.

Strategic use of the European dimension

Identification of the opportunities and incentives the European dimension
offered was quickly followed by the decision to fully exploit them by turning
the politics of self-government into a 'three-level game'. The foremost
example is provided by the SNP's move to place its secession strategy in a
European context and use those aspects of the EU discussed above as a two-
pronged rhetorical argument underpinning it. From 1988 onwards, the
party campaigned on a policy of 'independence in Europe' based on the
guarantee that an independent Scotland would be a member state of the
European Union. This appears to have been a calculated move by the SNP
based on the realisation that the European dimension gave a structural
advantage to their independence policy vis-à-vis the status quo and, to a lesser
extent, devolution. The evidence suggests that the opportunity to reduce the
economic costs of secession was the most important factor behind the SNP's
strategy, but the institutional incentives played an even more prominent 'pre-
sentational' role. The SNP exploited them to claim that the new, Europeanised, version of independence had a much more favourable costs/
benefits balance than the version proposed in the 1970s. By placing independence in the context of the EU, the SNP shifted its constitutional policy
towards the centre of the political spectrum and succeeded in making it – and
the party – look mainstream. The 'mainstreaming' of independence and the

strategic advantage it gave the SNP produced two effects. First, all the other actors were forced to respond to this challenge and play the game on the European level too. This meant adding a European dimension to their respective constitutional policies with Labour and the other devolutionist actors exploiting those aspects perceived to facilitate devolution. The evidence indicates that the representation incentive and the 'Europe of the Regions'/subsidiarity legitimation opportunity were those most exploited. Moreover, second, the devolutionist actors, led by the Labour party, also shifted their own policies closer to the SNP's by campaigning for a tax-varying Parliament and by signing up to the notion of Scottish popular sovereignty within the context of the Constitutional Convention.

The overall result was that the politics of self-government was in the 1990s clearly also played on an additional level, one which gave the SNP and, to a lesser extent, Labour and the other devolutionist actors, a structural advantage vis-à-vis the Conservatives, producing a neat reversal of the 1970s situation. The impact this had on the pattern of party competition determined that in this period Labour's devolution policy was developed in competition with the SNP's 'independence in Europe' policy against the Conservatives' policy of retaining the status quo. In contrast with the 1970s, the conflict intensity was by then clearly higher between the pro- and anti-self-government fronts than within the former as the united Yes-Yes organisation in the 1997 referendum campaign openly demonstrated. Additionally, the very principle of regional self-government appeared by then to be part of the zeitgeist. The anti-self-government camp employed the same tactic successfully used in 1979, i.e. tried to exploit the link between devolution and secession, but this time failed to shift public preferences in any significant way. The 'mainstreaming' of independence also led to the decision by the business organisations, in stark contrast with 1979, to keep a low profile during the campaign and not to invest resources in the No side. As discussed in chapter 7, business was in the 1990s no more hostile to independence than it was to devolution. The non-mobilisation of business was an important factor in depriving the No campaign of resources and credibility.

Mass public

As in the 1970s, elite agency was very effective in re-shaping public opinion to the extent that public support for the EU became widespread while the idea of 'independence in Europe' became popular well beyond Nationalist identifiers. In turn, the rise of independence to become both the second most preferred constitutional option and 'second best' among devolutionists neutralised the 'interaction effect' and cleared the way for a large Yes vote in the referendum.

Positive perception of the EU

As at the elite level, public attitudes to the EU were more complex in the 1990s than in the earlier period. In addition to the traditional economic dimension, there was by then an emerging social dimension shaping the perception of the EU. Attitudes to the economic dimension changed dramatically among Labour and Nationalist identifiers which led to economic integration being favourably perceived across the board. In contrast, the emerging social dimension was supported by those on the centre-left of the political spectrum but strongly rejected by Conservative identifiers. As this dimension grew in visibility and salience, its influence in shaping how the EU was perceived also grew. Support for the EU became by and large associated with the demand for self-government and a split attitude – positive on the 'economic' but negative on the 'social' – became associated with opposition to devolution. This also led, in a neat reversal of the 1970s situation, to pro-self-government voters clearly perceiving the EU as a 'positive alternative' to the UK rather than as a 'negative extension'. The elite actors' success in influencing public opinion was a necessary step in their strategy of utilising the European dimension to strengthen the demand for self-government as it would have been impossible for them to do so had the EU still been perceived in negative terms by the Scots. In the case of the SNP, in particular, it would have been virtually impossible to rally support around its policy of 'independence in Europe' if 'Europe' had not been perceived as a better alternative to Britain. As mass public awareness of European issues was limited, elite agency was crucial in re-shaping public opinion.

High support for independence

The changed perception of the EU among pro-self-government voters, and among Nationalist identifiers in particular, and the 'mainstreaming' of independence that it produced went a long way in re-configuring the distribution of constitutional preferences. The whole preference distribution shifted markedly towards the independence end of the spectrum with a tax-varying Parliament being the modal preference and 'independence in Europe' being the second-most-preferred option. Moreover, independence became 'second best' among devolutionists – especially Labour identifiers – reversing, once again, the pattern of the 1970s. The impact of the European dimension on this is clearly displayed by the variation between support for secession from both the UK and the EU, which only increased by two percentage points between 1979 and 1997, and support for secession from the UK *but* retention of membership of the EU, which increased by 26 percentage points, within overall support for independence rising five-fold to 35 per cent. The exploitation of the European dimension by the elite actors thus had the greatest impact on support for independence rather than for devolution.

Interaction effect neutralised

The fact that independence was by 1997 preferred to the status quo by those supporting devolution had the effect of neutralising the 'interaction effect' between devolution and independence that had caused the rejection of devolution in 1979. This was so despite the fact that devolution was still perceived to be likely to lead to independence. In the second referendum, however, all devolutionists preferring independence to the status quo – i.e. most of them – had nothing to lose by voting Yes. In the best scenario they would get their preferred constitutional status, in the worst scenario they would get independence but both scenarios were preferable to the default condition in the first place. This, coupled with the fact that many more voters supported independence outright, produced the end result that the gap between support for devolution and the referendum vote was minimal.

Conclusions

The politics of Scottish self-government was deeply Europeanised in the 1990s and this goes a long way towards explaining why devolution was endorsed in 1997 while it had been rejected eighteen years before. Europeanisation started with a sea-change in pro-self-government elite attitudes which turned them strongly pro-EU and led them to exploit the European dimension in their strategies in the context of a 'three-level game'. The successful exploitation of this extra dimension gave the procamp a structural advantage and enabled them to profoundly re-shape constitutional preferences at mass public level. Not only did support for the EU become widespread but 'independence in Europe' became the second most popular constitutional option and was preferred to the status quo by those supporting devolution. This rise in support for independence was thus of paramount importance, both directly and, especially, indirectly because it neutralised the 'interaction effect' that killed devolution in 1979. Through changed perceptions and elite agency, Europeanisation re-shaped public opinion and opened the way for a large Yes vote in the 1997 referendum.

The macro-hypotheses listed in chapter 1 thus find empirical support as far as the 1990s are concerned. It is possible to reject the null hypothesis on the evidence that Europeanisation did have a profound impact on the politics of self-government in the 1990s and on producing the variation relative to 1979. On the grounds that continued hostility towards the EU and refusal to place independence 'in Europe' would have still made secession unacceptable and produced the 'interaction effect', it could indeed be claimed that Europeanisation was a necessary though not a sufficient condition for the endorsement of devolution in the 1997 referendum. Most micro-hypotheses – and the theoretical claims in the literature on which most of them are based – are also supported by these findings with the notable exceptions of the impact of Europeanisation on collective identities and, to a lesser extent, of the direct – as opposed to indirect – role of the structural funds in fuelling demands for regional self-government. Above all, the hypothesised connection with independence – and via independence indirectly on devolution – rather than directly on devolution itself finds substantial evidence in its favour.

Part III
CONCLUSIONS

10
Explaining Europeanisation and devolution

What explains the radically different extents to which Scottish devolution was Europeanised in the 1970s and in the 1990s? Was the deepening of European integration the key factor? As discussed in the pages below, no single factor can fully account for the variation, several changes among actors and institutions at each of the three levels – European, British, Scottish – played a role. Two connected factors, though, stand out as having had the greatest impact. First, the ideological change among left-of-centre elite actors that was instrumental in changing their perception of the European Union and opening the way to their exploitation of the European dimension. Second, the 'systemic shift' between the position of the EU and the UK relative to Scotland, in terms of institutional features and policy output, that moved the EU closer to Scotland than the UK and made the former a 'positive alternative' to the latter in the eyes of Scots demanding self-government. Thus, it was not the deepening of integration per se, but how it interacted with change at the state level and what Scottish elite actors made of it, that made the difference.

Evolution of the EU political system

The European Union underwent a very significant transformation between the two periods. The transformation is captured symbolically in its very change of name from European Communities – more often called the Common Market – to European Union. As discussed below, not only were economic and political integration substantially widened and deepened but the EU's policy output also shifted significantly to the left. The latter aspect, in particular, played a crucial role in the politics of self-government in Scotland.

Widening and deepening of economic integration

The EU internal market expanded considerably as a result of successive enlargements from nine to fifteen states. By 1997, the EU covered almost all of Western Europe thus creating a huge internal market of continental proportions. Moreover, the level of integration of this market deepened as a result of the single-market programme. Its provisions, drafted and enacted primarily between 1988 and 1992, intended to eliminate most technical barriers to cross-border trade and increase the ease of movement for both capital and labour. As regards capital movements, this trend was further deepened by the process of monetary union under way from about 1992 onwards. Taken together, these changes constituted a substantial change in the direction of turning the EU from little more than a free-trade area into an integrated single market. Although its level of integration was still far lower – for reasons of cultural heterogeneity and jurisdictional fragmentation – than that of an internal market of a federal state such as the US, let alone a unitary one such as Japan, the transformation was of considerable significance. The widening and deepening of the EU's internal market meant that cross-border economic activities had a much higher level of guarantees in the 1990s than twenty years before. This was a crucial aspect to the scenario in which a border could be established between the rest of the UK and Scotland, if the latter chose independence. In other words, the widening and deepening of economic integration further reduced the economic costs associated with secession and lent credibility to the SNP's claim that there were no economic costs but significant benefits in their policy of 'independence in Europe'.

Widening and deepening of political integration

Political integration also widened and deepened considerably, in three main ways. First, the territorial expansion of the EU, already mentioned, through 'Western' enlargements and the commitment to further expansion eastwards. The EU became unequivocally the dominant supra-national political organisation in Europe and the latter became increasingly associated with the former. Integration also widened in a functional sense, through the inclusion of important new policy areas, hitherto entirely run at the state level, within the competences of the EU. Environmental policy, justice and home affairs and foreign policy and defence are but the most glaring examples of this trend. The widening of the EU's policy remit had the effect of also producing a 'deepening' of integration with the Union and the state level getting increasingly close and interconnected. This produced a perception of the two levels being increasingly 'fused' whereas in the 1970s they were still seen as largely separate. The large percentage of state legislation constituted by transposition of European law and the rising importance of the European Council in the EU's institutional structure, are perhaps the most emblematic examples of this 'two-way' intermeshing taking place. The combined effect of these trends was to raise the importance of the EU as a policy-making forum, hence of representation in its decision-making institutions and processes. Given the continuing pre-eminence of the Council and the rise of the European Council, the focus was on representation in these institutions while the expectations that regions could play a significant role quickly died out after the Committee of the Regions, set up in 1994, failed to live up to the expectations of its advocates. These changes significantly raised the saliency of the representation of Scottish interests at the Union level and created a specific incentive for the acquisition of a self-government capacity. In the eyes of many, moreover, they reinforced the attractiveness of 'state' status vis-à-vis 'region' status for Scotland as only the former would have given Scotland direct representation in the European Council and the Council of Ministers. This offered Labour and, especially, the SNP the opportunity to claim that the need to represent Scotland effectively at the Union level was a key reason for demanding self-government.

Leftward shift in policy output

If the widening and deepening of economic and political integration have been widely noted and discussed, the same cannot be said of the changing political nature of the EU's policy output. The EU had for a long time been charac- terised by policies of so-called 'negative integration' – essentially market liber- alisation – which were perceived by the Left to have a right-wing bias. Over the 1980s, this changed considerably as a result of further development of the regional and environmental policies and the emergence of a whole new 'social dimension' to the single-market programme. Regional policies grew to become the second item of expenditure for the EU in the 1990s, while the social dimension acquired a particularly high profile, especially in the UK, as being almost as important as the economic dimension in defining the nature of the European Union. The 'regionalist' dimension of the EU's policy output was further emphasised by the fact that the process of integration became increasingly associated with the idea of a 'Europe of the Regions' and the principle of subsidiarity. In that scenario, regional governments would acquire a pre-eminent position in the multi-level EU system and the distribution of power and competences within the latter would reflect a preference for the lowest level possible. This association went beyond the mere rhetorical level and took concrete institutional manifestations such as the establishment of the

Committee of the Regions and, especially, the enshrining of subsidiarity in the Maastricht treaty. Although, as mentioned above, these ideas were at their most powerful in the early 1990s and faded somewhat afterwards, they remained influential throughout the decade. These developments moved the policy output and, to a lesser extent, the philosophical foundations of the Union leftwards and played a crucial role in dispelling the image of the EU as a capitalist and centralist organisation. By becoming a more 'friendly' political system in the eyes of left-of-centre opinion, the EU was offering the opportunity to add a positive external dimension to the demand for regional self-government. This was seized upon by the SNP, Labour and their allies to bolster their strategies against the constitutional status quo.

Evolution of the UK political system

Like the EU, the UK political system also changed profoundly between the two periods. It goes without saying that these changes were closely linked to the Conservative rule that characterised those years. Three trends, in particular, had a crucial impact on the politics of self-government in Scotland: a shift to the right in public policy, a process of centralisation and a growing sense at the elite level in Scotland of a 'democratic deficit'.

Rightward shift in policy output

Under the Conservative governments led by Margaret Thatcher, UK's public policy shifted markedly to the right as a result of aggressive reforms in the social, regional and fiscal fields in particular. In the social field, labour legislation was liberalised and the influence of the trade unions significantly curtailed. The whole 'balance of power' between labour and business was altered to the latter's advantage. These reforms went hand in hand with a radical revision of regional policy. The overall commitment to a re-balancing of the uneven pattern of British economic development was abandoned and support for declining industries was stopped in favour of a much more targeted support for inward investment. A wide-ranging process of privatisation got under way. The impact of these reforms was particularly strong in Scotland, where a large section of the workforce was employed in large industries dependent, in one way or another, upon government intervention. The Conservative reforms of national and, especially, local taxation also featured prominently in this rightwards trend. The core principles were simplification of taxation and a general lightening of the fiscal burden but one of the key consequences was the reduced progressivity of the system. The poll tax, introduced in Scotland one year ahead of England, was the most extreme example of this. The effect of this shift to the right was to move the UK's policy output further and further away from Scotland's preferences where a broad left-of-centre consensus deeply opposed to this reform remained dominant. This offered the pro-self-government camp the opportunity to claim that the constitutional status quo was no longer meeting Scotland's public policy needs.

Centralisation

A similar trend took place in the area of constitutional reform and central–local relations. The Conservative governments embarked on a process of re-centralisation of the UK system, marked in particular by the emasculation of local government and explicit opposition to the idea of regional government. The traditional freedoms of local government in areas such as housing and education were progressively reduced in the context of a generalised assertion of central control. The abolition of the Greater London Council in 1984 was the most emblematic example of this process. Equally determined was the Conservatives' opposition to regional government, not only for England but also for Scotland, Wales and Northern Ireland. The negative outcomes of the 1979 referendums were interpreted as a popular rejection of the principle of devolution – as well as, more specifically, of the respective Acts – and the issue was effectively removed from the political agenda. This process of centralisation and disregard for Scotland's demands affected the nature of the union between Scotland and England as the traditional nature of the UK as union-state appeared to be under threat. This offered the opportunity to some in Scotland to claim that the respect of the latter's prerogatives and specificities enshrined in the Act/Treaty of Union had been violated by the Conservative governments.

'Democratic deficit'

The impact on Scotland of the trends discussed above was, of course, exacerbated by the fact that at each general election from 1979 onwards, the Conservative party was consistently rejected by Scottish voters. The party was, moreover, in a more or less constant trend of decline and Conservative identifiers became fewer and fewer north of the border. In the eyes of some, the Conservatives had ceased to be a British party and had become a purely English party, if not an English nationalist one. In sum, the rightwards and centrewards shifts in the UK system, persistently rejected at each election in Scotland, had the effect of creating a widespread feeling, especially at the elite level, of a 'democratic deficit' in the UK under which the sovereignty of the Scottish people was regularly frustrated by the constitutional structure of the UK. This had the effect of delegitimising the status quo and was an important factor in re-shaping party competition on self-government against the latter.

Systemic shift of the UK and the EU relative to Scotland

The changes at the European and the British level outlined above had far-reaching consequences for the respective positions of the EU and UK political systems relative to Scotland's, amounting to a 'systemic shift'. Three main aspects are crucial here. First, the progressive democratisation of the European Union and its embrace of some elements of the 'Europe of the Regions' idea, coupled with its confederal character and the small-state bias of its institutional structure contrasted with the drive towards centralisation and disregard of regional–national specificities taking place within the UK. Moreover, the increasing visibility of the European dimension lent much greater visibility to the various processes of regional devolution under way in several other European states over the same period of time. This made the European 'model' both in terms of the EU itself and of several of its component states, appear closer and more attractive for a would-be self-governing Scotland than what had become a 'centralised, self-serving super-state'.[1] Likewise, secondly, the leftwards shift in EU public policy contrasted with the movement in the opposite direction of the UK policy output. In sum the policy output and the institutional structure of the UK moved further away from the preferences of the median Scottish voter while the EU's ones moved much closer. In particular, the EU ceased to be seen to be 'to the right' of the UK and became to be seen as being 'to its left'. Hence, left-of-centre opinion abandoned its erstwhile hostility and began to favour it while right-of-centre opinion became increasingly 'sceptical'. This shift was perceived, of course, to be even sharper in Scotland, because public opinion and elite actors in the country had long been – at least since the mid-1960s – 'to the left' of the UK as a whole. Thirdly, as discussed above, this opened the way for the pro-self-government actors in Scotland to place their demands in a Europe-wide framework and to associate them with the process of integration. A number of incentives and opportunities offered by the European dimension could then be exploited to reduce the costs and increase the benefits of Scottish self-government and thus raise its attractiveness. The EU ceased to be a 'negative extension' of the UK and became a 'positive alternative' to it. According to Campbell Christie, it was the almost simultaneous shift in opposite directions of the policy outputs of the UK and of the EU which fundamentally changed the perception of the latter in Scotland. In Christie's own words, with the development of EU social policy, 'we saw progress being made via Europe and not via Westminster . . . it [the EU] was seen as a means of by-passing these constant built-in right-wing majorities that we had at Westminster'.[2] More broadly, as Kenyon Wright put it: 'increasingly, the European Union became to be seen as our defender against Westminster rather than a greater enemy'.[3]

The crucial period in which this systemic shift took place and led to a re-positioning of party strategies and a re-shaping of public opinion was between 1983 and 1988. In 1983 the alignment was still the same as in 1979, in 1988 it had acquired the '1990s' features. Indeed, the high point of the Europeanisation of Scottish self-government was the 1987–92 Parliament, which was also, not by coincidence, the period in which the process of European integration was perceived as taking a giant leap forward and public support for European integration reached a peak across Europe. Even though the peculiar conditions of that period later changed or disappeared, the re-shaping of perceptions, attitudes and strategies remained largely unchanged until 1997 (figure 10.1).

Evolution of Scottish actors

The changes in the 'two-level institutional structure' in which Scottish actors operated, however, could only be brought to bear fruit if the actors themselves were able to exploit them. As pointed out in chapter 1, I consider actors' agency the key intervening variable linking structural features of the EU and the UK political systems and the distribution of preferences and opinions at mass public level. Crucial in this respect is how the patterns of incentives, opportunities and constraints institutional structures present are 'filtered' by actors' perceptions, themselves determined by their set of values, principles, beliefs etc. In this light, the following sections identify and discuss the key changes which took place among Scottish actors between the two periods.

Ideological change

As discussed in part I of the book, ideology loomed large in the politics of Scottish self-government in the 1970s, and in the failure to Europeanise it in particular. Ideological change is thus essential to understanding the variation in this respect between the 1970s and the 1990s. The crucial change was that the key pro-self-government elite actors – the SNP, Labour and the STUC – underwent a deep process of ideological revision in relation to two central

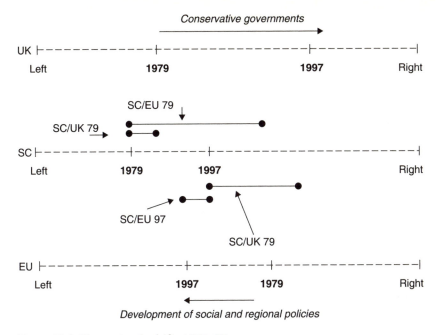

Figure10.1 The systemic shift, 1979–97

Note: This figure attempts to provide a graphic illustration of the perceived positions of the UK and the EU political systems in relation to Scotland's at the time of the two referendums and display the 'systemic shift' that took place in the 'dynamic period' 1979–97. The horizontal lines describe the positions of the three political systems on a left/right axis with the vertical intersections representing the positions of the three systems. UK, SC and EU stand for the UK, Scotland and the EU, respectively. The graph makes three points. First, that the UK system moved rightwards over the period, 1979–97 – as a result of Conservative policies – while the EU system moved leftwards – as a result of the development of social and regional policies. Second, Scotland moved in the same direction as the UK but it was to the left of the latter both in 1979 and in 1997. The results of these pattern of positions and movements is that the 'distance' – the continuous lines with solid circles at the end – between Scotland and the EU was greater than that between Scotland and the UK in 1979 while the reverse was true for 1997.

issues: the nature of national sovereignty and the role of government in the economy. As regards the former, the revision concerned both a 'relativisation' of the idea of sovereignty and a re-discovery of its democratic roots. Perceptions of sovereignty increasingly moved away from a monolithic conception and the idea that sovereignty can be pooled or vertically segmented became widely accepted. Contextually, the idea that sovereignty within Scotland rested with the Scottish people rather than with the UK Parliament gained equally wide acceptance. This revision was instrumental in leading the SNP to abandon its maximalist position of secession from the UK *and* the EU and to reconstruct its constitutional policy around the idea of 'independence in Europe' and in leading the Labour party and a wide range of interest groups in signing up to the notion of sovereignty of the Scottish people as embodied in the *Claim of Right* of 1988. As regards the role of government in the economy, the revision led to a wide acceptance of a liberal 'economic constitution' as a framework for managing contemporary European economies and thus to a profound re-consideration of the economic role of governments. Taken together these two aspects of the ideological revision of the 1980s had the effect of dramatically changing the perception of economic integration and of the supra-national character of the European Union among nationalist and left-of-centre opinion in Scotland. Indirectly, but crucially, it also changed the perception of those features of the EU system which had remained constant over time. Two properties of the EU that figured prominently in the pro-self-government discourse of the 1990s but were ignored in the 1970s – the customs union and the small-state bias – were not new, they had been there since at least 1968, when the customs union was completed. Conversely, many of the features of the EU that aroused most hostility in the 1970s, such as the agricultural and fisheries policies and the opacity of the decision-making process, changed little between the two periods.

Identificational change

Of deep significance also was the change in collective identities, with the decline in primary identification with the UK and the concomitant rise in primary identification with Scotland. This was particularly sharp among Labour identifiers who, as seen above, were also the only group of party identifiers whose voting pattern changed significantly between the two referendums. Moreover, primary identification with Scotland was a stronger determinant of the referendum vote in 1997 than in 1979, in line with the convergence of 'class' and 'nation' thesis put forward by Denver et al. Though this evolution in collective identification does not appear to have been directly linked to the change in attitudes towards the European Union[4] – as seen above – it did have important consequences for the Europeanisation of Scottish devolution. This was so because the further rise of a primary Scottish identity altered the balance between the 'affective' and the 'utilitarian' perception of the UK in Scotland, by weakening the former and emphasising the latter.[5] The utilitarian perception was based on a 'contractual' approach through which 'membership' of the UK was viewed increasingly on the basis of its 'utility' to Scotland in competition with other institutional arrangements. As this utility declined with the UK's move away from median Scottish preferences, the attraction of other options – chiefly of direct membership of the

European Union – increased. If the European dimension reduced the economic and political costs of a separation from the rest of the UK, the fading of the 'affective' identification with Britain reduced the 'emotional' costs of such a move. In sum, the decline in primary identification with the UK left Scottish perceptions of the British Union more liable to be influenced by the European dimension.

Generational change

Lastly, change among Scottish actors was also brought about, of course, by generational renewal. A new generation of leaders took control of the SNP, the Labour party and the STUC and was instrumental in changing their attitudes to the European dimension and their strategies on self-government. Some of them physically embodied the link between the two levels acting simultaneously at the Scottish and at the European level. The SNP's Winnie Ewing, for instance, one of the most charismatic leaders of the party, was elected to the European Parliament for the Highlands and Islands constituency in 1979 and would become a long-serving MEP. The STUC's secretary, Campbell Christie, made 'Europe' a top priority of his leadership and was an influential member of the EU's Economic and Social committee for a long time. Other figures, such as Gordon Wilson and Jim Sillars in the SNP and John Smith in Labour, also played a crucial role in Europeanising the demand for self-government in the 1990s. What is remarkable about these leaders is that most of them had been bitterly hostile towards the EU in the 1970s. While it is possible to read a constructivist dynamics in these 'conversions' to 'Europe' as a result of 'institutional learning' through membership in, or familiarity with, the EU's institutions, the evidence emerging from the interviews is that the decision to 'play the European card' was mostly a 'cold', rational decision based on a careful calculation of the costs and benefits involved. The difference with the earlier period was that the lifting of the 1970s 'ideological fog' cleared the way for a rational assessment of the European dimension to take place and shape consequential strategic decisions.

Europeanisation and devolution

As reviewed in chapter 1, although no explicitly comparative study of the two referendums has so far been carried out and no comprehensive explanation for the difference in results has been advanced, it is possible to identify three main explanatory accounts in the literature. The first is centred on the content of the two devolution packages as represented by the Scotland Act 1978 and the *Scotland's Parliament* 1997 white paper, respectively. According to this thesis, the former was perceived as an overwhelmingly partisan document intended to entrench Labour domination in Scotland through an assembly elected by the first-past-the-post system. In contrast, the 1997 white paper was the product of a wide consensus within Scottish society, symbolised by the agreement on a proportional electoral system. The partisan nature of devolution in 1979 produced a partisan pattern of voting whereby non-Labour pro-devolutionists – notably Conservative identifiers – turned against the Scotland Act in the run-up to the referendum. In contrast, the consensual nature of the 1997 proposals ensured a broad and steady support for devolution up to and at the referendum.[6]

The second explanation focuses on the degree of unity and the popularity of the Labour party and the effectiveness of the pro-devolution referendum campaign. It points out that Labour was divided and deeply unpopular in 1979 and that the Yes campaign was divided and under-funded relative to their opponents.[7] In contrast the Labour party was united and at the peak of its popularity in September 1997, the Yes campaign was also united and it enjoyed higher financial resources than the No side.[8] These differences determined that in 1979 Labour's unpopularity and the ineffective campaign undermined support for devolution while in 1997 the situation was reversed.

The third, and currently most influential, argument focuses on the role of the 'democratic deficit' created by eighteen years of Conservative rule at the UK level which was consistently rejected in Scotland. According to this theory, demand for self-government was 'soft' in the 1970s and was thus easily defeated by the Conservative policy of supporting devolution in principle but opposing the Scotland Act 1978 in practice.[9] In contrast, the 1979–97 'democratic deficit' had transformed home rule into the 'settled will of the Scottish people', which was reflected in very stable public support for devolution.[10] Different authors account for this either in terms of a convergence of the 'class' and 'identity' cleavages or as the 'mobilisation of the middle classes'.[11] In all these accounts, the connection between attitudes to devolution and attitudes to independence is almost totally neglected while the European dimension receives some attention but is not analysed in detail.[12]

While most of these explanations certainly point to important factors in the dynamic of the demand for devolution in Scotland between 1979 and 1997, they are unable, either individually or collectively, to provide a satisfactory general explanation for the different results of the two referendums, either empirically or theoretically. The claim that the Scotland Act 1978 was rejected because non-Labour identifiers perceived it as Labour-biased is not confirmed by the pattern of referendum voting by party identification.

Although a significantly larger proportion of Conservative than Labour identifiers voted No, Liberal identifiers displayed a voting pattern not very different from Labour's and Nationalist identifiers voted overwhelmingly Yes (table 4.3).[13] Nor is it consistent with the fact that a substantial proportion of Labour identifiers themselves also voted No. Put another way, only 51 per cent of those voters who, despite favouring devolution in principle, voted No to the Scotland Act 1978 were Conservative identifiers.[14] Moreover, the voting patterns of non-Labour identifiers were very similar in the two referendums. This evidence is inconsistent with the claim that the Scotland Act 1978 was rejected because it was perceived as biased in favour of Labour while the White Paper 1997 was not. Likewise, the hypothesis that devolution did not get enough support in 1997 because it was associated with an unpopular government does not find support in the data. The fundamental problem here is that the claim of Labour's unpopularity derives from UK-wide opinion surveys rather than data relative to Scottish opinion.[15] As the 1979 general election results relative to October 1974 indicate, Labour's popularity increased in Scotland, with the party gaining 5 per cent in votes and three additional MPs. Moreover, attitudes towards the Labour government – as proxied by support for Prime Minister Callaghan – were not significantly correlated with the referendum vote and did not have an independent impact on the latter (table 4.12).

It is more difficult to validate or refute the hypothesis that devolution was rejected in 1979 because of the fragmentation and lack of resources of the Yes campaign and endorsed in 1997 on the strength of the Yes campaign. It is likely that the relative strength of the campaigns had a significant influence on the outcomes. However, this explanation misses the crucial point that, notwithstanding a decline in support during the campaign in January and February 1979, support for self-government was still above 60 per cent at the time of the referendum (table 4.2). Like the previous one, this account thus fails to explain why a large proportion of Scots who were theoretically in favour of devolution voted No and why almost half of them did so despite identifying with parties supporting devolution.

The 'democratic deficit' thesis itself does not fully stand up against the empirical evidence. If we accept that support for devolution was higher in 1997 than in 1979 as a result of the 'democratic deficit', we should expect four phenomena to have occurred between 1979 and 1997: a sharp decline in satisfaction with the UK government among non-Conservative identifiers, dissatisfaction with the UK government being a stronger determinant of demand for self-government in 1997 than in 1979, a higher importance of self-government as a political issue and, most of all, higher support for devolution itself. However, there is no evidence that these phenomena occurred.

First, the second sharpest decline in satisfaction with the UK government took place among Conservative identifiers while Nationalists were actually more satisfied in 1997 than in 1979 (tables 4.10 and 8.7). Secondly, trust in the UK government was not an independent determinant of the demand for self-government in 1997 (table 8.9). Thirdly, the perceived importance of self-government as a political issue actually declined between 1979 and 1997 across all groups of party identifiers (tables 4.1 and 8.1). Lastly, but most importantly, support for devolution fell from 54 to 43 per cent (tables 4.2 and 8.2).

In sum, though it is certainly true that the 1997 white paper was a more consensual document than the Scotland Act 1978, that the pro-self-government campaign was more compact and better organised in 1997 than in 1979 and that there was a distinct feeling of 'democratic deficit' at elite level in the 1990s, these factors do not explain why the perceived importance of self-government at mass public level did not increase, nor why support for devolution actually fell, let alone why a Scottish assembly was rejected in 1979 when 60 per cent of voters favoured it in principle.

In contrast, the Europeanisation model presented and discussed in this book is able to capture the diachronic change in the politics of Scottish self-government between the 1970s and the 1990s and to provide a theoretically coherent and empirically supported explanation for the different results of the two referendums.

Conclusions

Five main conclusions are at the heart of the argument presented in this book. First, Europeanisation was virtually absent in the 1970s. Although a number of features of the EU system potentially offered opportunities and incentives for Scottish self-government and could have been exploited to that effect by the elite actors pursuing it this did not happen. By and large, elite actors perceived no positive connections between the European dimension and their demand for self-government, primarily because they had a deeply negative opinion of the European Union. In turn, their hostility to the EU was to a large extent a function of their ideological positions. Mirroring perceptions and discourse at the elite level, hostility to the EU and a negative association between support for self-government and support for the EU was widespread at mass public level. Because of the existence of a deep hostility towards independence and the preference for the status quo as a second best among devolutionists, an 'interaction effect' was generated which turned majority support for devolution into a rejection of the Scotland Act in the 1979 referendum.

In the 1990s, on the other hand, the politics of Scottish devolution was heavily Europeanised. Elite actors pursuing self-government had positive attitudes to the EU and fully exploited the European dimension in their strategies. Attitudes to the EU – especially its social dimension – were also positive at the mass public level and, moreover, were broadly associated with the demand for self-government. Because independence was by then placed 'in Europe' it enjoyed much higher support than in 1979, especially among non-Nationalist identifiers. Independence became 'second best' over the status quo among devolutionists so no 'interaction effect' was generated. High support for devolution was neatly translated into a strong Yes vote in the referendum. Europeanisation was thus two-fold: direct and indirect. The former impacted on support for devolution directly while the latter impacted on it indirectly, via support for independence and the 'interaction effect'. The evidence suggests that the indirect impact was more powerful than the direct one.

The process of Europeanisation of Scottish devolution thus worked through three key causal mechanisms. First, the existence of a close connection between attitudes to devolution and attitudes to independence with the potential to create an 'interaction effect' between the two. Depending on the shape of the preference distribution between devolution, independence and the status quo, this interaction effect could be 'destructive', i.e. undermining support for devolution via hostility to independence. The connection between attitudes to the two self-government options had itself been created by the fact that independence was not as such an option put to the vote but it was widely perceived to be facilitated by the setting up of a devolved assembly/Parliament. Secondly, perceptions of independence vis-à-vis the status quo and devolution were strongly influenced by attitudes to the international environment, of which the European dimension was the most important element. Whether or not independence was placed in the context of the EU and whether or not the latter was perceived as a positive institutional environment, were crucial variables shaping support for secession. Thirdly, elite actors' agency was the key intervening variable between the 'two-level institutional structure' constituted by the EU and the UK, and opinion at mass public level. Elite discourse and mobilisational strategies had the ability to shape public opinion and were utilised to that effect to exploit the European dimension in the 1990s. When elite perceptions and strategies changed, change at mass public level quickly followed.

The differential Europeanisation of Scottish devolution can be explained by a number of independent and intervening variables that changed between 1979 and 1997, as discussed in this chapter. If all of these variables had an impact, two in particular were of paramount importance. The first was the movement in opposite direction of the EU and the UK political systems that produced a 'systemic shift' in their relations to Scotland's. This profoundly changed the nature of the 'two-level structure' in which Scotland was nested and led to a wide-ranging re-alignment of attitudes and strategies. The second was the ideological change affecting elite actors. This lifted the 'ideological fog' that had prevented them from seeing the opportunities and incentives the European dimension was offering and was equally crucial in shaping a re-alignment of attitudes and strategies. Counter-intuitively, therefore, it was not the deepening of integration per se which was key but other aspects which tend to be rather overlooked in the literature.

While the existing contributions to the literature point to important aspects of the politics of devolution in the 1970s and in the 1990s, they do not provide a unified and comprehensive explanation for the different results of the two referendums. This is so because no explicitly comparative study has been conducted and, especially, because existing works overlook four crucial factors: the interaction between attitudes to devolution and attitudes to independence, the role of the European dimension in shaping attitudes to independence, the gap between support and vote in 1979 and the decline in support for devolution between 1979 and 1997. These factors feature prominently in the model presented and discussed in this book. Based on a cross-time comparative analysis of both elite actors and public opinion, the model is able to explain why devolution was defeated in 1979 despite majority support and why it was endorsed in 1997 even though support fell in the intervening period. The book thus offers an in-depth analysis of the degree to which Scottish devolution was Europeanised from the 1970s to the 1990s and provides a theoretically coherent and empirically substantiated account for the different outcomes in 1979 and 1997.

Lastly, this analysis of the Scottish case sheds new light on the theoretical question of the connections between the process of European integration and the demands for regional self-government. As seen in the introductory chapter, the question has been present in the literature since at least the mid-1970s and is naturally at the heart of the sub-field now labelled Europeanisation but had not yet been subjected to rigorous theoretical and empirical scrutiny. The Scottish case suggests that Europeanisation has the potential to deeply influence the politics of regional self-government in the EU states and that, under certain conditions, its influence is positive, i.e. it tends to strengthen the demand for self-government. Whether it does so however depends, crucially, on the agency of elite political actors who, to a large extent, control the channels through which the European dimension filters down to the regional level. This is consistent with the stress recent literature on Europeanisation places on political actors' agency[16] and opens stimulating avenues for further comparative research to arrive at a general theoretical model of how Europeanisation impacts on regional demands for self-government.

Notes

1 *Scotland's Parliament, Scotland's Right*, p. 31.
2 Christie, interview with the author; see also Aitken (1997: 299–300).
3 Wright, interview with the author.
4 See also Dardanelli (2002: 240–1).
5 On the long-standing co-existence of the two approaches in Scotland, see Keating (1978) and Fry (1978: 166).
6 Balsom and McAllister (1979: 402–5), Mitchell et al. (1998: 168).
7 Watt (1979: 146), Bochel and Denver (1981: 144), Butler and McLean (1999:7) and Kellas (1999: 225) emphasise the unpopularity of the Labour party, Perman (1979: 54), Mitchell (1996: 163–4), Mitchell et al. (1998: 167) and Denver et al. (2000: 19) stress the divisions and the contradictions within the Yes campaign.
8 See Jones (1997: 3–4); Mitchell et al. (1998: 168); Pattie et al. (1998: 14–5); Pattie et al. (1999: 141–2); Denver et al. (2000: 49, 75–6).
9 Bochel and Denver (1981: 144) and Brand (1986: 38).
10 See Brown et al. (1998: 62), Mitchell et al. (1998: 178), Pattie et al. (1998: 14), Pattie et al. (1999: 140), Kellas (1999: 223), Paterson and Wyn Jones (1999: 179–80), Surridge and McCrone (1999: 440), Taylor (1999: xxxix–xl), Denver et al. (2000: 169).
11 Denver et al. (2000: 28–32) emphasise the former while Paterson et al. (1992: 634), Paterson and Wyn Jones (1999) and Surridge and McCrone, (1999: 44), emphasise the latter.
12 See Brown et al. (1998: 64–5).
13 While these differences may be interpreted as being primarily determined by partisanship, they are also consistent with the fact that Conservative and Liberal identifiers were more strongly opposed to independence than Labour ones (table 4.7).
14 See Dardanelli (2002: 336).
15 See Denver et al. (2000: 159).
16 See, among others, Börzel and Risse (2003) and contributions to Fallend et al. (2003).

11

Epilogue: a new Scotland in a changing Europe

This last chapter turns its attention away from the past and into the future. It offers some reflections on Scotland's place in the European Union in the post-devolution period and the likely influence that the European dimension will continue to have on the issue of Scottish independence. It argues that the European dimension will continue to be very important for Scotland but that some of the exaggerated expectations about devolution's ability to provide a quantum leap in Scotland's relations with the EU have been and are likely to continue being disappointed. A more general disillusion with devolution and the devolved institutions is also evident across Scottish society and does not bode well for those who would like to gain more self-government. While the European dimension still offers theoretical incentives to acquire statehood, these are likely to be outweighed for the foreseeable future by powerful constraints.

Devolution six years on

Devolution has given Scotland the degree of self-government many of its citizens desired for a long time. As mentioned in chapter 6, according to the late John Smith, leader of the Labour party, devolution was the 'settled will of the Scottish people'. A Scottish Executive has taken over the former Scottish Office's machinery of government and is now accountable to a Parliament directly elected by an additional member system. Under the terms of the Scotland Act 1998, the devolved Parliament has a very wide range of policy competences – ranging from tourism to the legal system – while some matters are 'reserved' for Westminster competence. The devolved Parliament has become the focus for politics in Scotland and there is anecdotal evidence that the office of MSP is perceived to be more attractive than that of MP. As expected, the additional member system has not produced a single party majority in Parliament either in 1999 or in 2003 thus leading to the formation of a governing coalition between Labour and the Liberal Democrats. It has also benefited the Scottish National party, which has become the main opposition to the Lab–Lib coalition, and, somewhat less expectedly, the more extreme parties: the Conservatives on the right and the Scottish Socialists and the Greens on the left. The partisan make-up of the Parliament and the shape of the party system in Scotland thus differ significantly from the British ones. This difference, of course, was one of the aims of the devolutionists as expressed in the hope, for instance, that devolution would usher in a 'new style of politics' in Scotland that would even contribute to the reform of the British system of government. The very shape of the Parliament's chamber – a hemicycle rather than opposing benches – and its working methods were deliberately intended not to make it a copy of Westminster. The role of committees meant to empower backbenchers vis-à-vis the executive figured prominently in this respect. While the Parliament has made great strides in the direction of a 'working' Parliament rather than a 'debating' Parliament, achievements have somewhat fallen short of expectations.[1] The fact that governments of broadly the same political complexion have been in power in Edinburgh and London has also somewhat reduced the scope for policy divergence between Scotland and the rest of the UK, which was, of course, one of the fundamental raisons d'être of devolution. Nonetheless the executive has adopted policy initiatives that are significantly different from the UK ones, notably in the field of higher education and health. To a significant extent, therefore, devolution has started to fulfil the role its advocates hoped for.

At the level of public opinion, however, a certain disillusionment with devolution is evident and has shown up in electoral behaviour. Well over half of the electorate think devolution has made no difference to the way Scotland is governed and 50 per cent – up from 39 per cent in 1999 – think Westminster still has more influence on their lives than Holyrood. Turnout for the Scottish elections has been around 10 percentage points lower than for the general elections and has declined from 59 per cent in 1999 to 49 per cent in 2003.[2] It is probably fair to say that expectations of what devolution could achieve were extremely high so that a degree of disillusion was almost inevitable. Moreover, devolution has suffered from its association with a series of unfortunate events that have tarnished its image. Within three years of its establishment, the Scottish executive had already gone through three first ministers, following the death of the 'father of devolution' Donald Dewar in 2000 and the resignation in the wake of a corruption scandal of his successor Henry McLeish in 2001. Even more serious damage has been done by the 'saga' of the Parliament building, where criticisms have focused on the huge cost over-runs, the delays and the opaque decision-making process that led to its construction. It is likely that the negative effects that these 'teething problems' have had on devolution's image will gradually fade away as events become more distant in people's memory but for the time being they have played a significant role. Despite this devolution still commands widespread approval and no political force dares proposing its reversal. Indeed, public support for devolution has risen from 43 per cent in 1997 to around 54 per cent in 2003 while support for independence has dropped to 25 per cent.[3]

Relations with the EU

As seen throughout this book, the issue of Scotland's relations with the European Union has always loomed large in the politics of self-government, right from the day the UK joined the Union in 1973. Partly this was because Scottish elite actors tended to draw a distinction between European policy and foreign policy. The former was seen as more akin to domestic policy while the latter was associated with security and defence and as such beyond the limits of any devolution of power from Westminster. Although at the time few perceived the EU as a political system in its own right, even back in the 1970s there was widespread support for the proposed Scottish assembly to be involved in European policy. The prospect of European affairs being separated from foreign affairs and devolved to Scotland, however, always appeared a remote one, for it directly clashed with Westminster's desire to retain control of the full spectrum of international relations. Even the Constitutional Convention acknowledged that it was not realistic to demand the devolution of European policy. The maximum that could be achieved was obtaining the same rights enjoyed by regions in the EU federal states, such as the right to take part in the Council of Ministers when an issue affecting regional competences is on the agenda. Given this background, it is not surprising that under the Scotland Act 1998 European affairs are a reserved Westminster matter hence formally beyond reach of the Scottish Parliament and executive. The modus operandi of intra-UK inter-governmental relations concerning European policy, however, is more co-operative than the letter of the Act might suggest. The Memorandum of Understanding which is meant to regulate the relationship between Holyrood and Westminster acknowledges that efforts should be made to associate the Scottish institutions with the central government where matters affecting Scotland are concerned and Scottish ministers do have the right to represent the UK in the Council in those circumstances.[4] However, this matters more on a symbolic level than on a practical one. As is the case for the similar arrangements in place in

Belgium and Germany, regional ministers represent their state in the Council not their region/s. This is not usually a significant limitation for regional representatives of largely symmetrical systems – e.g. Belgium and Germany – because regional ministers represent the collective position of the regions which is unlikely to diverge significantly with the interests of the country as defined by the federal government. It is, however, in Scotland's case – given its asymmetrical devolution compared to Wales and the English regions – because it creates the potential that Scottish interests might significantly diverge from those of the UK as a whole and thus present Scottish ministers in the Council with a fundamental 'conflict of interests'. Moreover, as Wright argues, the right to sit in the Council itself does not represent a dramatic change with the past as Scottish Office ministers already had that right within the pre-devolution constitutional framework.[5] If devolutionists can reasonably claim that devolution has improved the representation of Scottish interests at the European level, other 'European' elements of their 1990s discourse appear to have lost some of their rhetorical power. The 'Europe of the Regions' concept is less potent than it used to be since it became clear, as discussed below, that no uniform regionalisation across Europe is possible and that there are fundamental differences between a 'region' such as the South-West of England and Bavaria or Catalonia or Flanders or, indeed, Scotland. References to a 'Europe of the Regions' have become somewhat marginalised in the official discourse of the EU institutions, the Committee of the Regions has failed to become a significant player and the principle of subsidiarity tends to be more narrowly confined to the relations between the Union and the states. Even more significantly, the overall perception of the EU in Scotland is less positive than it was in the 1990s as also shown by the decline in support for the adoption of the euro. While this mirrors the trend at the level of the UK as a whole, it is particularly significant for the perception of the EU as a 'positive alternative' to the UK. Such a perception has, of course, also been eroded by the fact that the UK's image in Scotland has improved as a result of several factors, including devolution itself, the similarity in policy output between Holyrood and Westminster, a certain rightwards shift in median preferences etc. In sum, it is likely that as the legitimation effect for devolution of the European dimension loses relevance, other aspects of the EU system might acquire greater saliency. In that respect, the EU may come to be seen more as placing constraints on the exercise of regional self-government than as offering opportunities and incentives for acquiring it.[6] This theoretically leaves a certain competitive edge to the independence option, though, as discussed below, formidable obstacles on that path remain.

Regionalism and secessionism across Europe

As seen in part II, the processes of regionalisation in other Western European countries and, to a lesser extent, of secession in some Eastern European countries had a significant 'demonstration effect' on the demand for self-government in Scotland in the 1990s. What is the situation across Europe in this respect in the mid-2000s? What does it imply for Scotland's constitutional status? As could be expected, there is no clear trend and no unequivocal answer. With regard to the creation or strengthening of a regional tier of government, a number of states that embarked on this path in the 1990s – or before – have gone further in this direction. Belgium has gone through a so-called fifth round of federalisation in 2001 with the transfer of some additional competences to the regions and pressures remain for going further in the area of social expenditure, which is still largely in the hands of the federal government.[7] Though collective identification with Belgium has increased in Flanders since the process of federalisation began, support for secession is still strong. The secessionist right-wing Flemish Bloc had grown relentlessly and was on the point of becoming the largest party in Flanders when it was ruled a racist organisation by the Court of Cassation. This deprived it of state funding and effectively forced the party to disband though the Bloc's leaders reacted by simply setting up a carbon-copy party named Flemish Interest. How this will affect the prospect for secession in Flanders is unclear at this stage. In France a new round of regionalisation is under way following the 2003 constitutional amendments which have, for the first time, enshrined the principle of decentralisation in the constitution. Also for the first time, limited legislative powers for the regions are envisaged, notably in areas where regional circumstances may differ significantly from the rest of the country, e.g. the presence of minority languages. Not much progress, on the other hand, has been made in finding a solution for Corsica's situation where a package of limited devolution was rejected in a referendum in July 2003. In Italy an ongoing process of decentralisation is also under way. After the transfer of more competences to the regions under the centre-left Prodi and D'Alema governments in 1997–99, the process is now taking a clearer federal profile with a new package of reforms, including the federalist transformation of the Senate, now in the process of parliamentary approval. Notwithstanding these moves, significant resistance to the progressive federalisation of Italy remains, including within the Berlusconi government which is currently pushing the reforms through. The Northern League, the main force behind this process of federalisation throughout the 1990s, remains an influential member of the ruling centre-right coalition but its 'blackmail potential' has arguably been weakened by the sidelining of its charismatic leader due to illness and the earlier abandonment of its secessionist discourse. In Spain, demands for more self-government are afoot in both the Basque Country and Catalonia in the context of a revision of the 1970s statutes of autonomy and are likely to find a more sympathetic hearing from the new socialist government than they did from the Aznar government. The secessionist Republican Left party has grown significantly in recent years and is now in the regional government although support for secession itself remains limited in Catalonia. The same could not be said of the Basque Country, where separatist feelings are still strong and where the Nationalist party in office at the regional level is planning a unilateral referendum on a package of reforms bordering on secession. If these cases might give the impression that the demand for regional self-government – both devolved and independent – is a rising tide sweeping Europe, it should be pointed out that regionalisation has also suffered significant defeats, notably in Portugal and, most recently, in England. In the former, the creation of a regional tier of government on the mainland was rejected in a referendum in November 1998 and no significant support for its resurrection exists at the time of writing. In the latter, the Labour government's plans for asymmetrical devolution in the English regions were resoundingly rejected at their first referendum test in the North-East in November 2004 and they now appear all but shelved for the foreseeable future.

As regards 'actual', as opposed to potential, secession, the largely peaceful disappearance of the USSR and Czechoslovakia were the success stories of the 1990s and the stories have continued into this decade with the building of solid democracies and thriving economies in most of the small new states created, such as Estonia and Slovakia. These could be interpreted as a demonstration that peaceful secession is possible and that small new states can thrive in the world, thus throwing a positive light on secession. On the other hand, the bloody fragmentation of Yugoslavia and the ongoing, seemingly intractable, problems in Bosnia, Kosovo and Macedonia also stand as a powerful reminder that secessions can trigger horrendous conflicts and generate long-lasting state- and nation-building difficulties. These cases have, of course, received much more public attention than the 'success stories' and have given a very negative connotation to secession. On balance, I would argue that the negative experiences since the 1990s have been more influential than the positive experiences in shaping public perception of secession. Therefore, though significant support for it exists in a number of regions, secession is still seen in a negative light across Europe and faces formidable obstacles in attracting majority support. In contrast, despite some setbacks, regionalisation is still marching on and is still seen in a largely positive light both on the left and on the right. In sum, in the 2000s Europe is still experiencing a broadly based phase of decentralisation of power, especially to a regional tier of government, but this has not spilled over into a trend towards state fragmentation.

The SNP strategy and the independence option

As mentioned above, the SNP is now the second party in Scotland and the clear alternative to the Lab–Lib ruling coalition. The achievement of independence is still the party's central aim, though it has been made, since 1997, conditional on endorsement by the Scottish people in a referendum. The European dimension still features as prominently in this strategy as it did in the 1990s. The aim is to become an additional member of the European Union and to exploit all the incentives and opportunities for acquiring statehood the EU systems offer. The latter have changed little over the last ten years. The single market is more integrated than it was then but only marginally so, hence economic factors have not dramatically changed. Likewise, the disproportionate influence that small states wield in the decision-making architecture of the EU is still largely in place, although one could argue that the Nice treaty and the new Rome treaty – the Constitutional treaty – have somewhat reduced it by giving greater power to the larger states, notably in the reformed qualified majority voting procedure in the Council. The SNP is thus still in a position to argue that independent statehood within the EU is the best constitutional option for Scotland in continuity with its position since 1988. Nonetheless, as mentioned above, the call for independence appears to resonate less strongly now than it used to do with Scottish voters. Devolution has given a very large degree of autonomous self-government to Scotland and has shifted the focus of Scottish politics away from constitutional issues and towards public policy and more day-to-day issues in general. Under the Swinney leadership, the party found it difficult to adapt to the new circumstances and at the same time to keep the beacon of independence alight. Following the setback of the 2003 election, when it lost 6 per cent of votes and eight seats relative to 1999, the charismatic Alex Salmond has made a comeback to the leadership of the party, in a move that can be interpreted as a knee-jerk reaction rather than a sign of a clear strategic direction. The building of the SNP's credibility as a party of government has still some way to go. Scotland's position as a net beneficiary of UK public expenditure and the 'friendly' relations between Edinburgh and London under Labour have also contributed to taking the edge off the party's appeal. This is reflected in the decline of public support for independence compared to 1997 which has raised the spectre that that long-standing fear of hard-line secessionists – that devolution would satisfy Scots sufficiently to postpone the achievement of independence indefinitely – might indeed have materialised.

Prospects

Despite the disillusion and the teething problems mentioned above, devolution can be a seen as a success and indeed as the 'settled will' of the Scottish nation. No significant actor, the Conservatives included, advocates a return to the pre-devolution constitutional arrangement. Furthermore, it is likely that with time the devolved institutions will take even more solid roots in Scottish society. The European dimension will remain very important for Scottish politics but no qualitatively significant change in the relationship between the Scottish institutions and their EU counterparts is likely to take place. Despite lobbying hard in the European Convention the so-called 'constitutional regions' have largely failed to have their demands for greater input into the EU's decision-making process accepted with the result that the Constitutional treaty leaves the status quo virtually unaltered.[8] This, as already mentioned, gives a theoretical advantage to statehood versus 'region-hood' for stateless nations such as Scotland but the advantage still appears to be dwarfed by the obstacles secession faces both in the European arena and in terms of SNP's abilities. Foreign policy is, to some extent, an area where the party might be able to build a distinctive profile for its independence option. If UK governments, especially future Conservative-led ones, continue to pursue a foreign policy at odds with the mainstream preferences of the Scottish people – as happened with the invasion of Iraq in 2003 – gaining control of foreign policy might acquire greater saliency for the electorate and thus boost the appeal of independence. However, under the circumstances that are likely to prevail in the foreseeable future it is difficult to see how independence can achieve majority support in Scotland. Moreover, even a major surge in support for the SNP would be unlikely, under the additional-member system, to give the party the chance to form a single-party secessionist government. The receding of the prospect of independence may in fact further undermine support for the party itself. The best forecast that can be formulated at this point in time is thus that independence will remain a distant prospect while devolution will embed itself more deeply in Scotland.

Notes

1 See Arter (2004).
2 See Boon and Curtice (2003).
3 Ibidem: 10 and, more broadly, Bromley and Curtice (2003).
4 See Wright (2003: 101–4).
5 Ibidem.

6 This interpretation is consistent with Börzel's (1999) and Bourne's (2003) findings in relation to Germany and Spain.

7 See Swenden (2003).

8 See Laible (2003).

Bibliography

Primary Sources

Archives

Scottish Conservative and Unionist party archive, National Library of Scotland, Edinburgh
Scottish Labour party archive, Mitchell Library, Glasgow
Scottish National party archive, National Library of Scotland, Edinburgh
Scottish Trades Union Council archive, Caledonian Library, Glasgow

Datasets

Miller, W. and J. Brand, *Scottish Election Study, 1979* [computer file]. Colchester, Essex: The Data Archive [distributor], 1981. SN: 1604
McCrone, D. et al. *Scottish Election Survey, 1997* [computer file]. 2nd ed. Colchester, Essex: The Data Archive [distributor], 24 June 1999. SN: 3889
Jowell, R. et al. *Scottish and Welsh Referendum Studies, 1997* [computer file]. Colchester, Essex: The Data Archive [distributor], 2 December 1998. SN: 3952.

Interviews

1   Campbell Christie. STUC general secretary 1986–98. Personal interview. 3 April 2000
2   Roseanna Cunningham. SNP MP for Perth and Kinross 1995–99. Personal interview. 30 March 2000
3   John Downie. Scottish Federation of Small Businesses. Personal interview. 14 July 2000
4   Lex Gold. Scottish Chambers of Commerce director. Personal interview. 3 April 2000
5   Allan Hogarth. Head of Public Affairs, Scottish CBI. Personal interview. 5 April 2000
6   Alasdair Hutton. Conservative MEP for South Scotland 1979–89. Personal interview. 31 March 2000
7   Bruce Millan. Labour Secretary of State for Scotland 1976–79, Shadow Secretary of State for Scotland 1979–83, European Commissioner for Regional Policy 1989–95. Personal interview. 31 March 2000

8   Ray Perman. Director, Scottish Financial Enterprise. Telephone interview. 26 July
    2000
9   Kevin Pringle. Spokesman for Alex Salmond, SNP leader since 1990. Personal
    interview. 4 April 2000
10 Malcolm Rifkind. Conservative Shadow Secretary of State for Scotland 1975–76,
    Secretary of State for Scotland 1986–90, Secretary of State for Transport
    1990–92, Secretary of State for Defence 1992–95, Secretary of State for Foreign
    Affairs 1995–97. Telephone interview. 27 March 2000
11 Norman Shanks. Convenor, Church and Nation Committee of the Church of
    Scotland, 1986–90. Telephone interview. 24 July 2000
12 Tom Sunter. Director, Scottish Institute of Directors. Personal interview. 13 July
    2000
13 Gordon Wilson. SNP Leader 1979–90. Personal interview. 30 March 2000
14 William Wolfe. SNP Leader 1968–79. Personal interview. 1 April 2000
15 Kenyon Wright. Secretary of the Scottish Constitutional Convention. Personal
    interview. 12 July 2000

Government documents

1973. *Report of the Royal Commission on the Constitution*. 31 October. Vol. I Report,
    Cmnd. 5460 and Vol. II Memorandum of dissent, Cmnd. 5460–1
1974. *Democracy and Devolution: Proposals for Scotland and Wales*. 7 September.
    Cmnd. 5732
1975. *Our Changing Democracy – Devolution to Scotland and Wales*. 22 November.
    Cmnd. 6348
1976. *Devolution to Scotland and Wales – Supplementary statement*. 1 August. Cmnd.
    6585
1976. *Scotland and Wales Bill*. 28 November.
1978. *Scotland Act*.
1997. *Scotland's Parliament*. July. Cm 3658

Other primary publications

1974. *Scotland Will Win with Labour*. Labour Party Scottish manifesto for the
    October general election. Glasgow: Scottish Council of the Labour Party
1975. *Reports to the General Assembly*. Edinburgh: Church of Scotland
1976. *Annual Report*. Glasgow: Scottish Trades Union Congress
1976. *Reports to the General Assembly*. Edinburgh: Church of Scotland
1977. *Annual Report*. Glasgow: Scottish Trades Union Congress
1977. *Reports to the General Assembly*. Edinburgh: Church of Scotland
1978. *Annual Report*. Glasgow: Scottish Trades Union Congress
1979. *Annual Report*. Glasgow: Scottish Trades Union Congress
1979. *The Bettor Way for Scotland*. Labour Party Scottish manifesto for the general
    election. Glasgow: Scottish Council of the Labour Party
1979. *Conservative Manifesto for Scotland*. Edinburgh: Scottish Conservative and
    Unionist Party
1979. *Reports to the General Assembly*. Edinburgh: Church of Scotland
1980. *Reports to the General Assembly*. Edinburgh: Church of Scotland

1982. *Reports to the General Assembly*. Edinburgh: Church of Scotland
1983. *Choose Scotland – the Challenge of Independence*. Scottish National Party manifesto for the general election. Edinburgh: Scottish National Party
1988. *A Claim of Right for Scotland*. Edinburgh: Campaign for a Scottish Assembly
1989. *Reports to the General Assembly*. Edinburgh: Church of Scotland
1990. *Towards Scotland's Parliament*. Edinburgh: Scottish Constitutional Convention
1991. *A Power for Change*. Glasgow: Scottish Trades Union Congress
1992. *The Best Future for Scotland*. Conservative Party Scottish manifesto for the general election. Edinburgh: Scottish Conservative and Unionist Party
1992. *Devolution and Independence Survey*. Edinburgh: Edinburgh Chamber of Commerce and Manufactures
1992. *General Council Report*. Glasgow: Scottish Trades Union Congress
1992. *It's Time to Get Scotland Moving Again*. Labour Party Scottish manifesto for the general election. Glasgow: Scottish Council of the Labour Party
1993. *General Council Report*. Glasgow: Scottish Trades Union Congress
1993. *Reports to the General Assembly*. Edinburgh: Church of Scotland
1994. *Action for Scotland in Europe*. Labour Party Scottish manifesto for the European election. Edinburgh: Scottish Conservative and Unionist Party
1994. *SNPower for Change*. Scottish National Party manifesto for the European election. Edinburgh: Scottish National Party
1994. *A Strong Britain in a Strong Europe*. Conservative Party Scottish manifesto for the European election. Edinburgh: Scottish Conservative and Unionist Party
1995. *Congress Programme*. Glasgow: Scottish Trades Union Congress
1995. *Scotland's Parliament, Scotland's Right*. Final report of the Scottish Constitutional Convention. Edinburgh: Scottish Constitutional Convention
1996. *General Council Report*. Glasgow: Scottish Trades Union Congress
1996. *Reports to the General Assembly*. Edinburgh: Church of Scotland
1997. *Because Scotland Deserves Better*. Labour Party Scottish manifesto for the general election. Glasgow: Scottish Council of the Labour Party
1997. *General Council Report*, Glasgow: Scottish Trades Union Congress
1997. *Reports to the General Assembly*. Edinburgh: Church of Scotland
1997. *Scottish Constitutional Reform – a Business Perspective*. Glasgow: The traser of Allander Institute for Scottish Chambers of Commerce
1997. *The Trades Union Agenda for a Scottish Parliament*. Glasgow: Scottish Trades Union Congress
1997. *Fighting for Scotland*. Conservative Party Scottish manifesto for the general election. Edinburgh: Scottish Conservative and Unionist Party
Eadie, Alex et al. 1974. *Scottish Labour and Devolution*. Glasgow: Scottish Council of the Labour Party

Memoirs, speeches and pamphlets

Dalyell, Tam. 1977. *Devolution – The End of Britain?* London: Jonathan Cape
Dalziel, Ian. 1980. Scotland in Europe. *Scottish Government Yearbook 1981*. Edinburgh: Harris
Herron, Andrew. 1989. Church and Nation: Turning Back the Clock! In Jock Stein (ed.), *Scottish Self-Government: Some Christian Viewpoints*. Edinburgh: The Handsel Press

Lindsay, Isobel. 1991. The SNP and the Lure of Europe. In Tom Gallagher (ed.), *Nationalism in the Nineties*. Edinburgh: Polygon

Mackintosh, John. 1982. *On Scotland*. Edited by Henry Drucker. London: Longman

Martin, David. 1992. *Towards a Wider, Deeper, Federal Europe*. London: The Fabian Society

Risk, C. 1978. Devolution – The Commercial Community's Fears. In Henry Drucker and M. Clarke (eds), *Scottish Government Yearbook* 1978

Sillars, Jim. 1986. *Scotland: The Case for Optimism*. Edinburgh: Polygon

Thatcher, Margaret. 1993. *The Downing Street Years*. New York: HarperCollins

Wolfe, Bill. 1973. *Scotland Lives*. Edinburgh: Reprographia

Wright, Kenyon. 1997. *The People Say Yes*. Glendaruel: Argyll Publishing

Secondary Sources

Aitken, Keith. 1997. *The Bairns O'Adam – The Story of the STUC*. Edinburgh: Polygon

Alesina, Alberto and Enrico Spolaore. 1996. *International Conflict, Defence Spending and the Size of Countries*. Working paper 5694. Cambridge, MA: National Bureau of Economic Research

Alesina, Alberto and Enrico Spolaore. 1997. On the Number and Size of Nations. *Quarterly Journal of Economics* 112/4: 1027–56

Alesina, Alberto and Romain Wacziarg. 1997. Openness, Country Size and the Government. *Journal of Public Economics* 69/3: 305–21

Anderson, James and James Goodman. 1995. Regions, States and the European Union: Modernist Reaction or Postmodern Adaptation? *Review of International Political Economy* 2/4: 600–31

Anderson, Jeffrey. 1991. Skeptical Reflections on a Europe of Regions: Britain, Germany and the ERDF. *Journal of Public Policy* 10/4: 417–47

Anderson, Perry. 1994. *The Invention of the Region*. Working paper RSC no. 94/2. Florence: European University Institute

Armstrong, Harvey. 1997. Regional-level Jurisdictions and Economic Regeneration Initiatives. In M. Danson (ed.), *Regional Governance and Economic Development*. London: Pion

Arter, David. 2004. The Scottish Committees and the Goal of a 'New Politics': a Verdict on the First Four Years of the Devolved Scottish Parliament. *Journal of Contemporary European Studies* 12/1: 71–92

Ashford, Nigel. 1980. The European Economic Community. In Zig Layton-Henry (ed.), *Conservative Party Politics*. London: Macmillan

Bache, Ian and Rachel Jones. 2000. Has EU Regional Policy Empowered the Regions? *Regional and Federal Studies* 10/3: 1–20

Balsom, Denis and Ian McAllister. 1979. The Scottish and Welsh Devolution Referenda of 1979: Constitutional Change and Popular Choice. *Parliamentary Affairs* 32/4: 394–409

Barker, Rodney. 1992. Legitimacy in the United Kigdom: Scotland and the Poll Tax. *British Journal of Political Science* 22/4: 521–33

Bartkus, Viva Ona. 1999. *The Dynamic of Secession*. Cambridge: Cambridge University Press

Bennie, Lynn, Jack Brand and James Mitchell. 1997. *How Scotland Votes.* Manchester: Manchester University Press

Birch, Anthony. 1978. Minority Nationalist Movements and Theories of Political Integration. *World Politics* 30/3: 325–44

Bochel, John and David Denver. 1981. The Outcome. In John Bochel, David Denver and Allan Macartney (eds), *The Referendum Experience: Scotland 1979.* Aberdeen: Aberdeen University Press

Bochel, John et al. 1981. The Background to the Referendum. In John Bochel, David Denver and Allan Macartney (eds), *The Referendum Experience: Scotland 1979.* Aberdeen: Aberdeen University Press

Bogdanor, Vernon. 1999. *Devolution in the United Kingdom.* Oxford: Oxford University Press

Bolton, Patrick and Gérard Roland. 1997. The Breakup of Nations: a Political Economy Analysis. *Quarterly Journal of Economics* 112/4: 1057–90

Bookman, Milica. 1993. *The Economics of Secession.* London: Macmillan

Boon, Martin and John Curtice. 2003. *Scottish Elections Research.* London: The Electoral Commission www.electoralcommission.org.uk/files/dms/ICMScottishElectionsreportfinal_9921-8023__E__N__S__W__.pdf

Borras-Alomar, Susana, Thomas Christiansen and Andres Rodriguez-Pose. 1994. Towards a 'Europe of the Regions'? Visions and Reality from a Critical Perspective. *Regional Politics and Policy* 4/2: 1–27

Börzel, Tanja. 1999. Towards Convergence in Europe? Institutional Adaptation to Europeanization in Germany and Spain. *Journal of Common Market Studies* 37/4: 573–96

Börzel, Tanja and Thomas Risse. 2003. Conceptualizing the Domestic Impact of Europe. In Kevin Featherstone and Claudio Radaelli (eds), *The Politics of Europeanization.* Oxford: Oxford University Press

Bourne, Angela. 2003. The Impact of European Integration on Regional Power. *Journal of Common Market Studies* 41/4: 597–620

Brand, Jack. 1986. Political Parties and the Referendum on National Sovereignty: the 1979 Scottish Referendum on Devolution. *Canadian Review of Studies in Nationalism* 13/1: 31–43

Bromley, Catherine and John Curtice. 2003. Devolution: Scorecard and Prospects. In Catherine Bromley et al. (eds), *Devolution – Scottish Answers to Scottish Questions?* Edinburgh: Edinburgh University Press

Brown, Alice, David McCrone and Lindsay Paterson. 1998. *Politics and Society in Scotland.* 2nd ed. Basingstoke: Macmillan

Butler, David and Iain McLean. 1999. Referendums. In Bridget Taylor and Katarina Thomson (eds), *Scotland and Wales: Nations Again?* Cardiff: University of Wales Press

Byrd, Peter. 1978. The Labour Party and the Trade Unions. In Martin Kolinsky (ed.), *Divided Loyalties.* Manchester: Manchester University Press

Cheshire, Paul. 1995. European Integration and Regional Responses. In Martin Rhodes (ed.), *The Regions and the New Europe.* Manchester: Manchester University Press

Connor, Walker. 1977. Ethnonationalism in the First World: The Present in Historical Perspective. In Milton Esman (ed.), *Ethnic Conflict in the Western World.* Ithaca, NY: Cornell University Press

Connor, Walker. 1984. Eco- or Ethno-Nationalism? *Ethnic and Racial Studies* 7/2: 342–59

Connor, Walker. 1994. *Ethnonationalism: the Quest for Understanding*. Princeton; NJ: Princeton University Press

Daniels, Philip. 1998. From Hostility to 'Constructive Engagement': The Europeanisation of the Labour Party. *West European Politics* 21/1: 72–96

Dardanelli, Paolo. 2002. *The Connection between European Integration and Demands for Regional Self-Government*. PhD thesis. London: London School of Economics

Davies, Norman. 1999. *The Isles – A History*. Basingstoke: Macmillan

Deacon, Susan. 1990. Adopting Conventional Wisdom: Labour's Response to the National Question. *Scottish Government Yearbook 1990*. Edinburgh: Harris

Dehousse, Renaud. 1996. *Intégration ou désintégration? Cinq thèses sur l'incidence de l'intégration européenne sur les structures étatiques*. Working paper RSC no. 96/4. Florence: European University Institute

Denver, David et al. 2000. *Scotland Decides – The Devolution Issue and the 1997 Referendum*. London: Cass

Dion, Stéphane. 1996. Why is Secession Difficult in Well-Established Democracies? Lessons from Quebec. *British Journal of Political Science* 29/2: 269–83

Drucker, Henry. 1978. *Breakaway: The Scottish Labour Party*. Edinburgh: EUSPB

Emizet, Kisangani and Vicki Hesli. 1995. The Disposition to Secede: An Analysis of the Soviet Case. *Comparative Political Studies* 27/4: 493–536

Fallend, Franz, Petra Grabner and Andrea Lenschow (eds) (2003). Europeanisation from an Actors' Perspective: The Taming of the Shrew? Special issue of the *Austrian Journal of Political Science* 32/3

Feld, Werner. 1975. Subnational Regionalism and the European Community. *Orbis* 18/4: 1176–92

Fry, Michael. 1978. Could Scotland Go it Alone? The Economic Factor in Devolution. *Round Table* 270: 166–71

Gabel, Matthew. 1998. *Interests and Integration: Market Liberalization, Public Opinion and European Union*. Ann Arbor, MI: University of Michigan Press

Garmise, Shari. 1997. The Impact of European Regional Policy on the Development of the Regional Tier in the UK. *Regional and Federal Studies* 7/3: 1–24

Garry, John. 1995. The British Conservative Party: Divisions over European Policy. *West European Politics* 18/4: 170–89

Geekie, Jack and Roger Levy. 1989. Devolution and the Tartanisation of the Labour Party. *Parliamentary Affairs* 42/3: 399–411

Goetz, Klaus. 1995. National Governance and European Integration: Intergovernmental Relations in Germany. *Journal of Common Market Studies* 33/1: 91–115

Gourevitch, Peter. 1979. The Reemergence of 'Peripheral Nationalisms': Some Comparative Speculations on the Spatial Distribution of Political Leadership and Economic Growth. *Comparative Studies in Society and History* 21/3: 303–22

Graham, Robert and Mick McGrath. 1991. Organised Labour and Europe: An Investigation of British and Scottish Perspectives. *Scottish Government Yearbook 1991*. Edinburgh: Harris

Greenwood, John and David Wilson. 1978. The Conservative and Liberal Parties. In Martin Kolinsky (ed.), *Divided Loyalties*. Manchester: Manchester University Press

Hale, Henry. 2000. The Parade of Sovereignties: Testing Theories of Secession in the Soviet Setting. *British Journal of Political Science* 30/1: 31–56

Hannan, Michael. 1979. The Dynamics of Ethnic Boundaries in Modern States. In John Meyer and Michael Hannan (eds), *National Development and the World System*. Chicago: University of Chicago Press

Hearn, Jonathan. 2000. *Claiming Scotland*. Edinburgh: Polygon

Hechter, Michael. 1975. *Internal Colonialism: The Celtic Fringe in British National Development, 1536–1966*. London: Routledge

Hechter, Michael. 1992. The Dynamics of Secession. *Acta Sociologica* 35/4: 267–83

Hix, Simon and Klaus Goetz. 2000. Introduction: European Integration and National Political Systems. *West European Politics* 23/4: 1–26

Hooghe, Liesbet. 1996. Building a Europe with the Regions: The Changing Role of the European Commission. In Hooghe (ed.), *Cohesion Policy and European Integration: Building Multi-Level Governance*. Oxford: Oxford University Press

Hooghe, Liesbet and Gary Marks. 1996. 'Europe with the regions': Channels of Regional Representation in the European Union. *Publius* 26/1: 73–92

Hooghe, Liesbet and Gary Marks. 2001. *Multi-Level Governance and European Integration*. Lanham, MD: Rowman & Littlefield

Horowitz, Donald. 1981. Patterns of Ethnic Separatism. *Comparative Studies in Society and History* 23/2: 165–95

Ichijo, Atsuko. 2004. *Scottish Nationalism and the Idea of Europe*. London: Routledge

Jeffery, Charlie. 1994. *The Länder Strike Back: Structures and Procedures of European Integration Policy-Making in the German Federal System*. Discussion papers in Federal Studies no. FS94/4. Leicester: University of Leicester

Jeffery, Charlie. 1996. Regional Information Offices in Brussels and Multi-level Governance in the EU: a UK–German Comparison. *Regional and Federal Studies* 6/2: 183–203

Jones, Peter. 1997. A Start to a New Song: The 1997 Devolution Referendum Campaign. *Scottish Affairs* 21: 1–16

Kauppi, Mark. 1982. The Decline of the Scottish National Party, 1977–81: Political and Organizational Factors. *Ethnic and Racial Studies* 5/3: 326–48

Keating, Michael. 1978. Parliamentary Behaviour as a Test of Scottish Integration into the United Kingdom. *Legislative Studies Quarterly* 3/3: 409–30

Keating, Michael. 1988. *State and Regional Nationalism: Territorial Politics and the European State*. London: Harvester Wheatsheaf

Keating, Michael. 1992. Regional Autonomy in the Changing State Order: A Framework of Analysis. *Regional Politics and Policy* 2/3: 45–61

Keating, Michael. 1993. The Continental Meso: Regions in the European Community. In Laurence Sharpe (ed.), *The Rise of Meso Government in Europe*. London: Sage

Keating, Michael. 1995. Europeanism and Regionalism. In Barry Jones and Michael Keating, *The European Union and the Regions*. Oxford: Clarendon Press

Keating, Michael and David Bleiman. 1979. *Labour and Scottish Nationalism*. London: Macmillan

Kellas, James. 1989. *The Scottish Political System*. Cambridge: Cambridge University Press

Kellas, James. 1991. European Integration and the Regions. *Parliamentary Affairs* 44/2: 226–39

Kellas, James. 1992. The Scottish Constitutional Convention. *Scottish Government Yearbook 1992*. Edinburgh: Harris

Kellas, James. 1999. The Scottish Political System Revisited. In Bridget Taylor and Katarina Thomson (eds), *Scotland and Wales: Nations Again?* Cardiff: University of Wales Press

Kendrick, Stephen and David McCrone. 1989. Politics in a Cold Climate: The Conservative Decline in Scotland. *Political Studies* 37/4: 589–603

Kohler-Koch, Beate. 1998. *La renaissance de la dimension territoriale en Europe: entre illusion et réalité*. Working paper RSC no. 98/38. Florence: European University Institute

Kolinsky, Martin. 1981. The Nation-State in Western Europe: Erosion from Above and Below? In Leonard Tirey (ed.), *The Nation-State: The Formation of Modern Politics*. Oxford: Martin Robertson

Ladrech, Robert. 1994. Europeanization of Domestic Politics and Institutions: The Case of France. *Journal of Common Market Studies* 32/1: 69–98

Laible, Janet. 2003. Constitutionalizing a 'Europe with the Regions': Competing Visions of EU Regions in the European Convention. Paper presented at the 99th APSA Annual Meeting. Philadelphia, PA: 27–31 August

Lane, Robert. 1991. Scotland in Europe: An Independent Scotland in the European Community. In Wilson Finnie, C. M. G. Himsworth and Neil Walker (eds), *Edinburgh Essays in Public Law*. Edinburgh: Edinburgh University Press

Lecours, André. 2000. Ethnonationalism in the West: A Theoretical Exploration. *Nationalism and Ethnic Politics* 6/1: 103–24

Levy, Roger. 1986. The Search for a Rational Strategy: The Scottish National Party and Devolution 1974–79. *Political Studies* 34/2: 236–48

Lynch, Peter. 1996. The Scottish National Party and European Integration: Independence, Intergovernmentalism and a Confederal Europe. In Lynch, *Minority Nationalism and European Integration*. Cardiff: University of Wales Press

Lynch, Peter. 1998. Reactive Capital: The Scottish Business Community and Devolution. *Regional and Federal Studies* 8/1: 86–102

Macartney, Allan. 1981. The Protagonists. In John Bochel, David Denver and Allan Macartney (eds), *The Referendum Experience: Scotland 1979*. Aberdeen: Aberdeen University Press

McCrone, David. 1991. 'Excessive and Unreasonable': The Politics of the Poll Tax in Scotland. *International Journal of Urban and Regional Research* 15/4: 443–52

McCrone, David and Bethan Lewis. 1999. The Scottish and Welsh Referendum Campaigns. In Bridget Taylor and Katarina Thomson (eds), *Scotland and Wales: Nations Again?* Cardiff: University of Wales Press

Marks, Gary. 1992. Structural Policy in the European Community. In Alberta Sbragia (ed.), *Euro-Politics – Institutions and Policy-Making in the 'New' European Community*. Washington, DC: Brookings Institution

Marks, Gary. 1996. Exploring and Explaining Variation in EU Cohesion Policy. In Liesbet Hooghe (ed.), *Cohesion Policy and European Integration*. Oxford: Oxford University Press

Marks, Gary, Liesbet Hooghe and Kermit Blank. 1996b. European Integration from the 1980s: State-Centric vs. Multi-Level Governance. *Journal of Common Market Studies* 34/3: 341–78

Marks, Gary, Jane Salk, Leonard Ray and François Nielsen 1996. Competencies, Cracks and Conflicts: Regional Mobilization in the European Union. *Comparative Political Studies* 29/2: 164–92

Martin, Pierre. 1995. When Nationalism Meets Continentalism: The Politics of Free Trade in Quebec. *Regional and Federal Studies* 5/1: 1–27

Martin, Steve and Graham Pearce. 1993. European Regional Development Strategies: Strengthening Meso-Government in the UK? *Regional Studies* 27/7: 681–5

Maxwell, Stephen. 1991. The Scottish Middle Class and the National Debate. In Tom Gallagher (ed.), *Nationalism in the Nineties*. Edinburgh: Polygon

Mbadinuju, Chinwoke. 1976. Devolution: the 1975 White Paper. *Political Quarterly* 47/3: 286–96

Meadwell, Hudson. 1989. Ethnic Nationalism and Collective Choice Theory. *Comparative Political Studies* 22/2: 139–54

Meadwell, Hudson. 1993. Transition to Independence and Ethnic Nationalist Mobilization. In William Booth, Patrick James and Hudson Meadwell (eds), *Politics and Rationality*. Cambridge: Cambridge University Press

Meadwell, Hudson. 1999. Secession, States and International Society. *Review of International Studies* 25/3: 371–87

Meadwell, Hudson. 2001. Institutional Design and State Breaking in North America. In David Carment, John Stack and Frank Harvey (eds), *The International Politics of Quebec Secession*. Westport, CT: Praeger

Meadwell, Hudson and Pierre Martin. 1996. Economic Integration and the Politics of Independence. *Nations and Nationalism* 2/1: 67–87

Mény, Yves. 1986. The Political Dynamics of Regionalism: Italy, France, Spain. In Roger Morgan (ed.), *Regionalism in European Politics*. London: Policy Studies Institute

Miller, William. 1980. The Scottish Dimension. In David Butler and Dennis Kavanagh (eds), *The British General Election of 1979*. London: Macmillan

Miller, William et al. 1977. The Connection between SNP Voting and the Demand for Scottish Self-government. *European Journal of Political Research* 5/1: 83–102

Mitchell, James. 1990. *Conservatives and the Union*. Edinburgh: Edinburgh University Press

Mitchell, James. 1996. *Strategies for Self-Government*. Edinburgh: Polygon

Mitchell, James. 1998. The Evolution of Devolution: Labour's Home Rule Strategy in Opposition. *Government and Opposition* 33/4: 479–96

Mitchell, James, David Denver, Charles Pattie and Hugh Bochel 1998. The 1997 Devolution Referendum in Scotland. *Parliamentary Affairs* 51/2: 166–81

Morris, Peter. 1996. The British Conservative Party. In John Gaffney (ed.), *Political Parties and the European Union*. London: Routledge

Murkens, Jo Eric with Peter Jones and Michael Keating. 2002. *Scottish Independence – A Practical Guide*. Edinburgh: Edinburgh University Press

Nagel, Joanne and Susan Olzak. 1982. Ethnic Mobilization in New and Old States: an Extension of the Competition Model. *Social Problems* 30/2: 127–43

Nanetti, Raffaella. 1996. EU Cohesion and Territorial Restructuring in the Member States. in Liesbet Hooghe (ed.), *Cohesion Policy and European Integration*. Oxford: Oxford University Press

Newman, Saul. 1996. *Ethnoregional Conflict in Democracies: Mostly Ballots, Rarely Bullets*. Westport, CT: Greenwood Press

Orridge, Andrew. 1982. Separatist and Autonomist Nationalisms: the Structure of Regional Loyalties in the Modern State. In Colin Williams (ed.), *National Separatism*. Cardiff: University of Wales Press

Orridge, Andrew and Colin Williams. 1982. Autonomist Nationalism: A Theoretical Framework for Spatial Variations in Its Genesis and Development. *Political Geography Quarterly* 1/1: 19–39

Parks, Judith and Howard Elcock. 2000. Why Do Regions Demand Autonomy? *Regional and Federal Studies* 10/3: 87–106

Paterson, William. 1994. Britain and the European Union Revisited: some Unanswered Questions. *Scottish Affairs* 9: 1–12

Paterson, Lindsay and Richard Wyn Jones. 1999. Does Civil Society Drive Constitutional Change? The Case of Wales and Scotland. In Bridget Taylor and Katarina Thomson (eds), *Scotland and Wales: Nations Again?* Cardiff: University of Wales Press

Paterson, Lindsay, Alice Brown and David McCrone. 1992. Constitutional Crisis: The Causes and Consequences of the 1992 Scottish General Election Result. *Parliamentary Affairs* 45/4: 627–39

Pattie, Charles, David Denver, James Mitchell and Hugh Bochel. 1998. The 1997 Scottish Referendum: An Analysis of the Results. *Scottish Affairs* 22: 1–15

Pattie, Charles, David Denver, James Mitchell and Hugh Bochel. 1999. Settled Will or Divided Society? Voting in the 1997 Scottish and Welsh Devolution Referendums. In Justin Fisher et al. (eds), *British Elections and Parties Yearbook Vol. 9*. London: Cass

Perman, Ray. 1979. The Devolution Referendum of 1979. *Scottish Government Yearbook 1980*. Edinburgh: Harris

Petersen, William. 1975. On the Subnations of Western Europe. In Nathan Glazer and Daniel Moynihan (eds), *Ethnicity: Theory and Experience*. Cambridge, MA: Harvard University Press

Polèse, Mario. 1985. Economic Integration, National Policies and the Rationality of Regional Separatism. In Edward Tiryakian and Ronald Rogowski (eds), *New Nationalisms of the Developed West*. Winchester, MA: Allen & Unwin

Proctor, J. 1983. The Church of Scotland and the Struggle for a Scottish Assembly. *Journal of Church and State* 25/3: 523–43

Rhodes, Martin. 1995. Introduction: the Regions and the New Europe. In Rhodes (ed.), *The Regions and the New Europe*. Manchester: Manchester University Press

Rhodes, Roderick. 1973–74. Anaemia in the Extremities and Apoplexy at the Centre. *New Europe* 2/2: 61–77

Rokkan, Stein and Derek Urwin. 1982. Introduction: Centres and Peripheries in Western Europe. in Rokkan and Urwin (eds), *The Politics of Territorial Identity: Studies in European Regionalism*. London: Sage

Rothschild, Joseph. 1981. *Ethnopolitics: A Conceptual Framework*. New York: Columbia University Press

Rudolph, Joseph. 1977. Ethnic Sub-States and the Emergent Politics of Tri-Level Interaction in Western Europe. *Western Political Quarterly* 30/4: 537–57

Scheinman, Lawrence. 1977. The Interfaces of Regionalism in Western Europe: Brussels and the Peripheries. In Milton Esman (ed.), *Ethnic Conflict in the Western World*. Ithaca, NY: Cornell University Press

Seawright, David. 1999. *An Important Matter of Principle – The Decline of the Scottish Conservative and Unionist Party*. Aldershot: Ashgate

Shanks, Norman. 1996. Constitutions, Conventions and Values: The Scottish Churches and the Constitutional Debate. *Scottish Affairs* 16: 18–35

Sharpe, Laurence. 1993. The European Meso: An Appraisal. In Sharpe (ed.), *The Rise of Meso Government in Europe*. London: Sage

Smith, Anthony. 1979. Towards a Theory of Ethnic Separatism. *Ethnic and Racial Studies* 2/1: 21–37

Smith, Anthony. 1982. Nationalism, Ethnic Separatism and the Intelligentsia. In Colin Williams (ed.), *National Separatism*. Cardiff: University of Wales Press

Smyrl, Marc. 1997. Does European Community Regional Policy Empower the Regions? *Governance* 10/3: 287–309

Sowemimo, Matthew. 1996. The Conservative Party and European Integration, 1988–1995. *Party Politics* 2/1: 77–97

Surridge, Paula and David McCrone. 1999. The 1997 Scottish Referendum Vote. In Bridget Taylor and Katarina Thomson (eds), *Scotland and Wales: Nations Again?* Cardiff: University of Wales Press

Swenden, Wilfried. 2003. *Belgian Federalism*. London: Royal Institute of International Affairs www.riia.org/pdf/research/europe//Swenden_final.pdf

Taylor, Bridget. 1999. Introduction and Conclusions. In Bridget Taylor and Katarina Thomson (eds), *Scotland and Wales: Nations Again?* Cardiff: University of Wales Press

Thompson, Robert and Joseph Rudolph. 1989. The Ebb and Flow of Ethnoterritorial Politics in the Western World. In Joseph Rudolph and Robert Thompson (eds), *Ethnoterritorial Politics, Policy and the Western World*. Boulder, CO: Lynne Rienner

Tömmel, Ingeborg. 1998. Tranformation of Governance: The European Commission's Strategy for Creating a Europe of the Regions. *Regional and Federal Studies* 8/2: 52–80

Unwin, Derek. 1982. Conclusion: Perspectives on Conditions of Regional Protest and Accommodation. In Stein Rokkan and Derek Unwin (eds), *The Polities of Terentorial Identity: Studies in European Regionalism*. London: Sage

Van Houten, Pieter. 2001. Regional Assertiveness in Western Europe – a Statistical Exploration. Paper presented at the 29th ECPR Joint Sessions of Workshops. Grenoble: 6–11 April

Van Houten, Pieter. 2003. Globalization and Demands for Regional Autonomy in Europe. In Miles Kahler and David Lake (eds), *Governance in a Global Economy: Political Authority in Transition*. Princeton, NJ: Princeton University Press

Wallace, Helen and William Wallace. 1973. The Impact of Community Membership on the British Machinery of Government. *Journal of Common Market Studies* 11/4: 243–62

Ward, Hugh. 2000. If the Party Won't Go to the Median Voter, then the Median Voter Must Come to the Party: A Spatial Model of Two-Party Competition with Endogenous Voter Preferences. Paper presented at the 50th PSA Annual Conference. London: 10–13 April

Ward, Hugh and Patrick Dunleavy. 1991. Party Competition: The Preference Shaping Model. In Dunleavy, *Democracy, Bureaucracy and Public Choice*. London: Harvester Wheatsheaf

Ward, Hugh and Patrick Dunleavy. 1981. Exogenous Voter Preferences and Parties with State Power: some Internal Problems of Economic Models of Party Competition. *British Journal of Political Science* 11/3: 351–80

Watt, David. 1979. The March 1st Referendum. *Political Quarterly* 50/2: 145–7

Weigall, David and Peter Stirk (eds). 1992. *The Origins and Development of the European Community*. Leicester: Leicester University Press

Wittman, Donald. 1991. Nations and States: Mergers and Acquisitions; Dissolutions and Divorce. *American Economic Review* 81/2: 126–9

Wood, John. 1981. Secession: a Comparative Analytical Framework. *Canadian Journal of Political Science* 14/1: 107–34

Wright, Alexander. 2003. The Internationalization of Scottish Politics: Who Governs Scotland? In José Magone (ed.), *Regional Institutions and Governance in the European Union*. Westport, CT: Praeger

Zaller, John. 1992. *The Nature and Origins of Mass Opinion*. Cambridge: Cambridge University Press

Index